CW00391146

AAT

Technician Level 4

Unit 17
Implementing Auditing Procedures

WORKBOOK

1183/A01

British Library Cataloguing-in-Publication Data

A catalogue record for this book is available from the British Library.

Published by Foulks Lynch Ltd
Number 4
The Griffin Centre
Staines Road
Feltham
Middlesex
TW14 0HS

ISBN   0 7483 5118 3

Printed and bound in Great Britain by Ashford Colour Press, Gosport, Hants.

Foulks Lynch Ltd, 2001

Acknowledgements

We are grateful to the Association of Accounting Technicians, the Association of Chartered Certified Accountants, the Chartered Institute of Management Accountants and the Institute of Chartered Accountants in England and Wales for permission to reproduce past examination questions. The answers have been prepared by Foulks Lynch Ltd. The copyright to the questions remains with the examining body.

All rights reserved. No part of this publication may be reproduced, stored in a retrieval system, or transmitted, in any form or by any means, electronic, mechanical, photocopying, recording or otherwise, without the prior written permission of Foulks Lynch Ltd.

CONTENTS

PREFACE

This is the 2001 edition of the AAT workbook for Unit 17 – Implementing Auditing Procedures. The workbook includes the simulation provided by the AAT.

The workbook has been produced to complement our Unit 17 textbook and it contains numerous practice questions and tasks designed to reflect and simulate the work place environment. These are arranged to match the chapters of the textbook, so that you can work through the two books together.

The workbook also contains practice devolved assessments to prepare you completely for the assessment procedures which form part of your course.

Fully comprehensive answers to all questions, tasks and assessments are provided, with the exception of those which are designated as being specifically for classroom work.

You will find that completion of all the elements of this workbook will prepare you admirably for the assessments which you must carry out to pass Unit 17.

Class Activities

A feature of this workbook is the section at the end comprising Activities which are specially designed for classroom use. The answers to these are not included in the workbook but are reproduced in the **College Kit** which is available to college lecturers who adopt our material.

College Kits

In addition to the Textbooks and Workbooks, Foulks Lynch offers colleges adopting our material the highly popular **'College Kits'**.

The College Kits for units with a Devolved Assessment contain:

- additional Devolved Assessment material in looseleaf form which can be photocopied to provide practice classwork for students (much of this additional Assessment material is taken from the AAT's own Assessments); and

- the looseleaf answers to the class examples from the Workbooks.

These Kits are supplied at no extra cost and may be photocopied under the limited licence which is granted to adopting colleges.

TECHNICIAN STAGE

NVQ/SVQ LEVEL 4 IN ACCOUNTING

AAT SPECIMEN SIMULATION

IMPLEMENTING AUDITING PROCEDURES

(UNIT 17)

◈ FOULKS*lynch*

ASSOCIATION OF ACCOUNTING TECHNICIANS

DATA AND TASKS

INSTRUCTIONS

This simulation is designed to test your ability to implement auditing procedures.

The situation is set out on page 3.

The tasks to be completed are set out on pages 4 and 5.

Your answers should be set out in the answer booklet provided on pages 22 to 48. If you require additional answer pages, ask the person in charge.

You are allowed **four hours** to complete your work.

A high level of accuracy is required. Check your work carefully before handing it in.

Correcting fluid may be used but it should be used in moderation. Errors should be crossed out neatly and clearly. You should write in black ink, not pencil.

You are advised to read the whole of the simulation before commencing as all of the information may be of value and is not necessarily supplied in the sequence in which you might wish to deal with it. The simulation contains a large volume of data which you may need in order to complete the tasks. An indication of the time to be allowed for each task is given for further guidance and the amount of space allowed in the answer booklet should be indicative of the length of response expected and allows for candidates with larger writing.

You are reminded that you should not bring any unauthorised material, such as books or notes, into the simulation. If you have any such material in your possession, you should surrender it to the assessor immediately.

Any instances of misconduct will be brought to the attention of the AAT, and disciplinary action may be taken.

THE SITUATION

You are an audit senior employed by an accountancy firm. You are helping with the audit of ABC Ltd, a private limited company which runs four shops selling ice cream and confectionery. A junior member of staff, Jo Smith, is also involved in the audit. The year you are auditing ended on 30 September 1997.

Your manager has had a meeting with the client, and now has several tasks which she would like you to complete. These are set out on pages 4 and 5 of this booklet.

TASKS TO BE COMPLETED

1. Familiarise yourself with the client by reading the permanent information on pages 6 and 7 of this simulation and the manager's notes of a meeting with the client on page 8. Then update the Accounting Systems notes (reproduced in the answer booklet on pages 23 – 25) for the latest changes that have been made.
   (Allow 20 minutes to complete this task.)

2. Using the updated Accounting Systems notes, produce a working paper, using the blank pages of your answer booklet, which sets out:
   - the inherent risks in ABC Ltd;
   - the controls which are present in the accounting system;
   - the weaknesses in the accounting system.
   (Allow 30 minutes to complete this task.)

3. On the blank page of your answer booklet, set out the tests which you would carry out to seek to confirm the controls for stock and purchases which you identified at task 2.
   (Allow 10 minutes to complete this task.)

4. Materiality has been set at £15,000. Review the balance sheet on page 9 and set out on the blank page of your answer booklet which assets and liabilities should be audited, noting the audit objectives for each balance. You must state why you have chosen these balances.
   (Allow 15 minutes to complete this task.)

5. Because of the small number of trade creditors, your manager has established a sample size of 5 for trade creditors. Using the creditors' listing on page 10 set out the following on the blank pages of your answer booklet:
   - suggest which balances should be tested giving the basis of your selection;
   - note how the balances should be tested to confirm their accuracy;
   - note any further work that should be done to confirm that all creditors are accurately recorded.
   (Allow 20 minutes to complete this task.)

6. Using the blank page in your answer booklet, set out the substantive tests which should be undertaken to confirm the following:
   - the completeness and accuracy of sales;
   - the validity and accuracy of payroll.
   (Allow 15 minutes to complete this task.)

7. Jo Smith is new to auditing and your manager has asked you to explain some important auditing matters to him. Using the memo paper on pages 34 and 35 of your answer booklet write to Jo Smith explaining the following:
   - the purpose of audit sampling;
   - some possible ways of selecting a sample;
   - what to do if errors are found in a sample; and
   - Jo Smith's responsibilities regarding confidentiality and security of working papers whilst on the audit of ABC Ltd.
   (Allow 20 minutes to complete this task.)

8. You are helping with the audit of ABC Ltd's stock figure. Jo Smith has prepared a stock schedule to confirm that stock is valued at the lower of cost and net realisable value. This schedule is set out on page 36 of your answer booklet.

Use the purchase invoices on pages 11–15 of this booklet, and the information given on Jo Smith's stock schedule, and complete this schedule.

In addition you should produce a working paper on the blank page of your answer booklet which sets out the objectives, work done, results and conclusion regarding this work on stock, and notes any further work that should be performed.
(Allow 30 minutes to complete this task.)

9. You are helping with the audit of fixed assets. The schedule on page 38 of your answer booklet has been prepared by the client. Audit this schedule to confirm that depreciation has been correctly calculated, and additions have been correctly accounted for. The invoice for the addition to motor vehicles is given on page 16 in this booklet.

Mark the client's schedule on page 38 of your answer booklet, and note any errors you have discovered using the separate sheet of paper if necessary.
(NB you are not required to calculate any potential adjustment.)
(Allow 15 minutes to complete this task.)

10. You are auditing creditors and can assume that the following balances are to be tested:

	Balance £
Thornbury's	19,123
Juicy Juices	17,214
Nice Ice Ltd	19,111
Alf's Afters	17,283
Dairymen	12,480

Confirm these creditors by agreeing or reconciling them to the statements given on pages 17–19, and using the purchase ledger accounts on pages 20 and 21. Schedule the work done on the blank pages of your answer booklet showing the objective, work done, results and conclusion.
(Allow 30 minutes to complete this task.)

11. You are performing a test to check that purchases have been recorded in the correct period. Jo Smith has done some of the work which is scheduled on pages 42 and 43 of your answer booklet. Review this schedule and write your conclusion at the bottom of the page; if necessary note any further action that should be taken.
(Allow 10 minutes to complete this task.)

12. Using pages 44 and 45 of your answer booklet set out two points for inclusion in a management letter. Use the weaknesses identified in task 2.
(Allow 15 minutes to complete this task.)

13. At the end of the audit it has been decided that the audit report will be unqualified. Using the blank page in your answer booklet draft the opinion paragraph of the audit report that should be issued in accordance with SAS 600.
(Allow 10 minutes to complete this task.)

Client	ABC Ltd
Accounting date	30 September

Prepared by	AAS
Date	15/12/96
Reviewed by	AMM
Date	18/12/96

PERMANENT INFORMATION

HISTORY OF THE BUSINESS

ABC Ltd is a private limited company whose principal activity is the sale of ice cream and confectionery. It has been in operation for 10 years and runs four shops in the West of England within 30 miles of each other.

Shareholders – Philip Thompson (50%)
                Susan Thompson (50%) – Philip's wife

Directors –   Philip Thompson
              Susan Thompson

Turnover is around £500,000 per shop with a net profit of £40,000 for the combined business. One of the shops is owned by the company and valued at £150,000. The other premises are rented.

ACCOUNTING SYSTEMS

Computer environment
The computer uses Sage software. A hard copy is maintained of all entries into the computer. The password for access to the computer is known only to Philip and Susan. Whilst back up procedures are in place, Susan admits to forgetting to do this at times. There are no contingency plans should the computer fail.

Management accounts
Susan is responsible for the accounting function.

Monthly management accounts are produced by shop and by department (i.e. ice cream, chocolate, sweets, drinks). The system produces formatted Profit and Loss Account and Balance Sheet, detailed nominal ledger and aged creditors. Philip reviews the monthly management accounts.

Sales
All sales are cash sales. Cash is banked daily less incidental expenses and wages of Saturday staff. Invoices are kept for all incidental expenses. A reconciliation between the till roll and the cash in the till is performed daily by the manager of each shop.

Susan records sales from the till roll analysed between ice cream sales, and other sales and VAT.

Stock
There is an annual stock count performed at each shop. Throughout the year Philip keeps an eye on the level of stock so he knows what to order. The goods have a fairly short shelf life, and old or damaged stock is thrown away.

The annual stock count is valued by Susan using the latest invoice price. This is appropriate for the FIFO basis of valuation since stock has a short shelf life.

Client	ABC Ltd
Accounting date	30 September

Prepared by	AAS
Date	15/12/96
Reviewed by	AMM
Date	18/12/96

Purchases and payments

Orders are made by Philip.

Deliveries are all made to Main Street, Taunton. Philip checks them against the order and delivery note and keeps the delivery note for agreement to the invoice; there is no evidence of Philip's check. He then delivers the goods to the other shops. This occurs once a week.

When the invoice arrives, Susan matches it to the delivery note and enters it on to the computer. The invoice and delivery note are stapled together for filing.

All other expenses are recorded on the computer when the invoice arrives.

Susan agrees the purchase ledger balance to the statements received each month.

All cheques are made out and signed by Susan. Philip is a cheque signatory but rarely gets involved with this.

Susan performs a monthly bank reconciliation and maintains a manual purchase ledger control account.

Payroll

This is prepared by Susan using the computer.

There are 6 salaried staff including the directors, and 6 paid by the hour. They submit weekly time sheets which are signed as approved by the shop manager.

Saturday staff are paid in cash out of the till. All others are paid directly into their bank accounts.

The payroll is reviewed by Philip to identify any unusual amounts.

Client	ABC Ltd
Accounting date	30 September 1997

Prepared by	AMM
Date	1/10/97
Reviewed by	
Date	

Notes of meeting with Philip and Susan Thompson

Susan and Philip have had a reasonably good year, with similar results to last year, ie, turnover £2,000,000 and net profit £40,000 (see the balance sheet and profit and loss account on page 9).

They computerised the stock records at the start of the year. The records are updated by Philip when deliveries are received, and are linked to the tills so that sales of stock are automatically reflected in the stock records. Each month a stock check is done in each shop covering a proportion of the total shop, this confirms that the computer stock figure is correct; there have been no major discrepancies in the year.

The stock is valued by the computer at the latest invoice prices.

Philip has also been keeping a record of sales per staff hour at each shop to enable him to monitor the effectiveness of the staff.

ABC Ltd
Balance sheet as at 30 September 1997

Fixed Assets	£	£
Property	150,000	
Fixtures and fittings	50,000	
Equipment	20,000	
Motor vehicles	30,000	
		250,000
Current assets		
Stock	25,000	
Prepayments	8,000	
Bank	90,000	
	123,000	
Current liabilities		
Trade creditors	108,000	
Other creditors	12,000	
	120,000	
Net current assets		3,000
Total assets less current liabilities		253,000
Long term liabilities		(10,000)
		243,000
Share capital		100
Profit and loss account		242,900
		243,000

Summary profit and loss account for the year ended 30 September 1997

	£
Sales	2,000,000
Cost of sales	1,000,000
Gross profit	1,000,000
Expenses	960,000
Net profit	40,000

AGED CREDITORS - 30 September 1997

A/c no	Name	Balance	Current	1 Month	2 Months	3 Months	>3 Months
1	Simpsons Sweets	875	375	90	310	100	0
2	Dial a dairy	0	0	0	0	0	0
3	Thornbury's	19,123	10,478	6,000	2,645	0	0
4	Smithsons	1,012	1,012	0	0	0	0
5	Maritime	0	0	0	0	0	0
6	Triangles and Treats	5,187	0	5,187	0	0	0
7	Juicy Juices	17,214	2,500	6,790	5,150	2,774	0
8	Confection Kingdom	0	0	0	0	0	0
9	Laslow's	0	0	0	0	0	0
10	Farthingales	128	0	128	0	0	0
11	Nice Ice Ltd	19,111	7,500	7,870	3,741	0	0
12	Crème de la crème	2,878	0	0	2,878	0	0
13	Epic Ice Cream	0	0	0	0	0	0
14	Gingham's	157	0	0	157	0	0
15	Sally Smiths	941	350	0	591	0	0
16	Jonsons Ltd	1,500	1,500	0	0	0	0
17	Alf's Afters	17,283	5,600	5,900	2,678	3,105	0
18	Ffords Ltd	8,586	3,881	2,647	2,058	0	0
19	Lyons	100	0	100	0	0	0
20	Barry's Business	2,200	2,200	0	0	0	0
21	Mullins	427	427	0	0	0	0
22	XYZ Ltd	684	684	0	0	0	0
23	Calvi's	(3,947)	0	0	0	0	(3,947)
24	Delia's Drinks	1,207	0	1,207	0	0	0
25	Ashby's	854	0	0	854	0	0
26	Dairymen	12,480	3,672	4,153	4,655	0	0
		108,000	40,179	40,072	25,717	5,979	(3,947)

PURCHASE INVOICES

TRIANGLES AND TREATS

Invoice to:
ABC Ltd, Main Street, Taunton

VAT No. 123 3423 12
Date: 26/8/97
Invoice no. 124350

Description	Quantity	Unit Price	£
Belgian chocs	10	1.50	15.00
Flakes – family	25	0.78	19.50
Sugar mice	100	0.20	20.00
Chocolate mice	100	0.25	25.00
Toffee bars	50	0.40	20.00
Bag sweets	40	0.28	11.20
Fudge bars	80	0.55	44.00

Sub total   154.70
VAT @ 17.5%   27.07

£181.77

TOTAL DUE

Payment in 30 days to:	Triangles and Treats
	Seaside Way
	Burnham on Sea

Alf's Afters

VAT No. 546 2765 89

Invoice no. 1234

To: ABC Ltd, Main Street, Taunton
Date: 30/9/97

	Unit price	Net price
40 × Chocogrand	0.88	35.20
40 × Sunsational	0.33	13.20
Net total		48.40
VAT at 17.5%		8.47
Total due		56.87

Payment due in 30 days to
Alf's Afters
30 The Street
Bristol

◆ **FOULKS**lynch

PURCHASE INVOICES (CONTINUED)

FFORD'S LTD   27,   *Bilbo's*
Industrial Estate, Taunton

Invoice No 564738   *VAT   No   475*
9878 25   Inv. date: 5/9/97

To: ABC Ltd, Main Street, Taunton

	Quantity	Price per unit	Net	VAT	Total
Multipack lollies	20	1.25	25.00	4.38	29.38
Opal fruit lollies	80	0.65	52.00	9.10	61.10
Citrus lollies	40	0.70	28.00	4.90	32.90
VAT @ 17.5%—£18.38				Total due	£123.38

NICE ICE LTD
The Shires, Yeovil

VAT No   234 7658 98
Invoice no   3243-987
Invoice date: **17 Sept '97**

Unit Price	Description	Net Total
6.30	4L Citron × 2	12.60
6.10	4L Cornish × 4	24.40
6.00	4L Vanilla × 12	72.00
6.30	4L Coffee × 4	25.20
6.30	4L Chocolate × 5	31.50
		165.70
	VAT 17.5%	28.99
	DUE	£194.69

Please make payments in 30 days to:
NICE ICE LTD
The Shires
Yeovil

PURCHASE INVOICES (CONTINUED)

Crème de la crème

Unit 29, Hedge End, Illminster
Invoice no   154
Invoice date   13/8/97
Customer: ABC Ltd, Main Street, Taunton

	Quantity		Unit Price	Total
Yoghurt bars	8	packs	19.76/pack	158.08
Mixed tubs	250		0.27	67.50
Single tubs	250		0.25	62.50
			Sub total	288.08
			VAT @ 17.5%	50.41
			Payable	£338.49

VAT Registration number 756 9876 34

SALLY SMITHS

Invoice number: 254

17, Shoe Street, Summerset

Invoice date: 1 September 1997

	Quantity	Unit price	Net	VAT— 17.5%	Total
Mars	50	0.40	20.00	3.50	23.50
Twix	50	0.40	20.00	3.50	23.50
Teddy Bear Cones	20	1.00	20.00	3.50	23.50
Standard Cones	100	1.00	100.00	17.50	117.50
Fiesta Cone × 39	90	1.00	90.00	15.75	105.75
Carrier bags	1,000	17.10/1,000	17.10	2.99	20.09
		Total due		£46.74	£313.84

VAT Registration number: 231 769409

PURCHASE INVOICES (CONTINUED)

**NICE
ICE
LTD**
The Shires, Yeovil

VAT No   234 7658 98

Invoice no   3243-1879

Invoice date: 10 Sept '97

Unit Price	Description	Net Total
0.20	10 Scoop pots & lids × 1,500	300.00
0.13	5 Scoop pots & lids × 1,500	195.00
0.75	Large block—vanilla × 100	75.00
0.50	Medium block—vanilla × 50	25.00
		595.00
	VAT 17.5%	104.12
	DUE	£699.12

Please make payments in 30 days to:
NICE ICE LTD
The Shires
Yeovil

TRIANGLES AND TREATS

Invoice to:
ABC Ltd, Main Street, Taunton

VAT No. 123 3423 12
Date: 10/9/97
Invoice no. 125466

Description	Quantity	Unit Price	£
Belgium bars	100	0.50	50.00
Dark choc bars	100	0.50	50.00
White choc bars	100	0.50	50.00
Classic chocs	100	1.17	117.00
	Sub total		267.00
	VAT @ 17.5%		46.73
	TOTAL DUE		£313.73

Payment in 30 days to: **Triangles and Treats**
Seaside Way
Burnham on Sea

PURCHASE INVOICES (CONTINUED)

Delia's Drinks

12 The Park
Bristol

Invoice no: 3452
Invoice date: 22 Sept. 1997
VAT Reg. No.   123 2345 345

	Quantity	Price per unit	£
Small cans	1,500	0.21	315.00
Large cans	1,500	0.30	450.00
Orange juice – small	1,000	0.15	150.00
Orange juice – large	1,000	0.50	500.00
Iced tea	500	0.25	125.00
			1,540.00
		VAT @ 17.5%	269.50
			£1,809.50

MOTOR VEHICLE INVOICE

CLIVES CARS

Invoice no. 123546
Invoice date 15/5/97
VAT Reg. no 345 7635 87

Main Street, Taunton

To: ABC Ltd, Main Street, Taunton

	£
Sale of Golf VR6 Reg. no. M123AAT Chassis No. 1746358 First registered – 15/10/94	13,000.00
VAT @ 17.5%	2,275.00
	15,275.00

CREDITOR'S STATEMENTS

NICE
ICE
LTD
The Shires, Yeovil

VAT No   234 7658 98

STATEMENT

Date: 30 Sept '97

To: **ABC LTD, MAIN ST, TAUNTON**

Invoice date		Net	VAT	Gross
3243-23	12/7/97	1,519.57	265.93	1,785.50
3243-45	18/7/97	382.98	67.02	450.00
3243-67	26/7/97	1,281.28	224.22	1,505.50
3243-89	5/8/97	4,051.08	708.94	4,760.02
3243-91	13/8/97	2,646.79	463.19	3,109.98
3243-18	10/9/97	595.00	104.12	699.12
3243-98	17/9/97	165.70	28.99	194.69
3243-19	25/9/97	5,622.29	983.90	6,606.19

£19,111.00

Please make payments in 30 days to:
NICE ICE LTD
The Shires
Yeovil

Alf's Afters
VAT No. 546 2765 89
To: ABC Ltd, Main Street, Taunton

STATEMENT

Date: 30/9/97

	£
B/F from previous statement	11,683.00
Invoice 786	4,100.00
Invoice 957	1,443.13
Invoice 1234	56.87

Payment due in 30 days to   £17,283.00
Alf's Afters
30 The Street
Bristol

CREDITOR'S STATEMENTS (CONTINUED)

THORNBURYS

BLAKE HOUSE, BRISTOL   **STATEMENT 30/9/97**

To: ABC Ltd, Main Street, Taunton

Invoice no	Date	£
1017	08/06/97	2,500.00
1132	12/07/97	1,345.00
1157	21/07/97	1,300.00
1289	03/08/97	1,450.00
1345	18/08/97	2,345.00
Payment received		(2,500.00)
1567	25/08/97	2,205.00
1789	01/09/97	4,500.00
1891	12/09/97	3,245.00
1923	13/09/97	2,733.00
1990	30/09/97	1,354.00
		£20,477.00

Juicy Juices
The Square, Taunton

STATEMENT – ABC Ltd – 30/9/97

Invoice no.	Date	DR	CR	Balance
7689	01/06/97	1,000.00		1,000.00
7908	12/06/97	457.00		1,457.00
8907	18/06/97	1,500.00		2,957.00
9342	30/06/97	817.00		3,774.00
9567	03/07/97	2,500.00		6,274.00
9889	12/07/97	2,650.00		8,924.00
10456	04/08/97	1,800.00		10,724.00
10789	10/08/97	3,578.00		14,302.00
11537	28/08/97	1,412.00		15,714.00
11879	15/09/97	2,500.00		18,214.00

Amount due:

Current	1 month	2 months	3 months	Total
2,500.00	6,790.00	5,150.00	3,774.00	**£18,214.00**

CREDITOR'S STATEMENTS (CONTINUED)

Dairymen

The Farm, Yate, Bristol

STATEMENT – 30/9/97 – ABC Ltd, Main Street, Taunton

Invoice no.		£
00794	....	1,200.00
00888	....	2,350.00
00917	....	1,105.00
00989	....	1,553.00
01741	....	2,600.00
01878	....	1,071.00
02901	....	2,601.00
03141	....	1,980.00
		£14,460.00

PURCHASE LEDGER ACCOUNTS

Juicy Juices

Date	Invoice no.	Dr	Cr
01/06/97	7689		1,000.00
12/06/97	7908		457.00
18/06/97	8907		1,500.00
30/06/97	9342		817.00
03/07/97	9567		2,500.00
12/07/97	9889		2,650.00
04/08/97	10456		1,800.00
10/08/97	10789		3,578.00
28/08/97	11537		1,412.00
15/09/97	11879		2,500.00
30/09/97	Payment	1,000.00	
Balance		17,214.00	
		£18,214.00	£18,214.00

Dairymen

Date	Invoice no.	Dr	Cr
b/f 01/07			4,784.00
02/07/97	00794		1,200.00
10/07/97	00888		2,350.00
15/07/97	Payment	2,000.00	
21/07/97	00917		1,105.00
05/08/97	00989		1,553.00
15/08/97	01741		2,600.00
15/08/97	Payment	2,784.00	
03/09/97	01878		1,071.00
08/09/97	02901		2,601.00
15/09/97	03141		
Balance		12,480.00	
		£17,264.00	£17,264.00

PURCHASE LEDGER ACCOUNTS (CONTINUED)

Thornburys

Date	Invoice no.	Dr	Cr
08/06/97	1017		2,500.00
12/07/97	1132		1,345.00
21/07/97	1157		1,300.00
03/08/97	1289		1,450.00
20/08/97	Payment	2,500.00	
18/08/97	1345		2,345.00
25/08/97	1567		2,205.00
01/09/97	1789		4,500.00
12/09/97	1891		3,245.00
13/09/97	1923		2,733.00
Balance		19,123.00	
		£21,623.00	£21,623.00

IMPLEMENTING AUDITING PROCEDURES

ANSWER BOOKLET

THE PAGES FOR YOU TO ANSWER THE INDIVIDUAL TASKS ARE AS INDICATED. IT IS ANTICIPATED THAT SUFFICIENT SPACE IS PROVIDED FOR ANSWERS. HOWEVER, A COUPLE OF SPARE PAGES ARE PROVIDED AT THE BACK OF THIS BOOKLET FOR USE IF NECESSARY.

ANSWERS (Task 1)

Client	ABC Ltd
Accounting date	30 September

Prepared by	AAS
Date	15/12/96
Reviewed by	AMM
Date	18/12/96

PERMANENT INFORMATION

HISTORY OF THE BUSINESS

ABC Ltd is a private limited company whose principal activity is the sale of ice cream and confectionery. It has been in operation for 10 years and runs four shops in the West of England within 30 miles of each other.

Shareholders – Philip Thompson (50%)
Susan Thompson (50%) – Philip's wife

Directors – Philip Thompson
Susan Thompson

Turnover is around £500,000 per shop with a net profit of £40,000 for the combined business.
One of the shops is owned by the company and valued at £150,000. The other premises are rented.

ACCOUNTING SYSTEMS

Computer environment
The computer uses Sage software. A hard copy is maintained of all entries into the computer. The password for access to the computer is known only to Philip and Susan. Whilst back up procedures are in place, Susan admits to forgetting to do this at times. There are no contingency plans should the computer fail.

Management accounts
Susan is responsible for the accounting function.

Monthly management accounts are produced by shop and by department (i.e. ice cream, chocolate, sweets, drinks). The system produces formatted Profit and Loss Account and Balance Sheet, detailed nominal ledger and aged creditors. Philip reviews the monthly management accounts.

ANSWERS (Task 1, continued)

Client	ABC Ltd
Accounting date	30 September

Prepared by	AAS
Date	15/12/96
Reviewed by	AMM
Date	18/12/96

Sales

All sales are cash sales. Cash is banked daily less incidental expenses and wages of Saturday staff. Invoices are kept for all incidental expenses. A reconciliation between the till roll and the cash in the till is performed daily by the manager of each shop.

Susan records sales from the till roll analysed between ice cream sales, and other sales and VAT.

Stock

There is an annual stock count performed at each shop. Throughout the year Philip keeps an eye on the level of stock so he knows what to order. The goods have a fairly short shelf life, and old or damaged stock is thrown away.

The annual stock count is valued by Susan using the latest invoice price. This is appropriate for the FIFO basis of valuation since stock has a short shelf life.

ANSWERS (Task 1, continued)

Client	ABC Ltd
Accounting date	30 September

Prepared by	AAS
Date	15/12/96
Reviewed by	AMM
Date	18/12/96

Purchases and payments

Orders are made by Philip.

Deliveries are all made to Main Street, Taunton. Philip checks them against the order and delivery note and keeps the delivery note for agreement to the invoice; there is no evidence of Philip's check. He then delivers the goods to the other shops. This occurs once a week.

When the invoice arrives, Susan matches it to the delivery note and enters it on to the computer. The invoice and delivery note are stapled together for filing.

All other expenses are recorded on the computer when the invoice arrives.

Susan agrees the purchase ledger balance to the statements received each month.

All cheques are made out and signed by Susan. Philip is a cheque signatory but rarely gets involved with this.

Susan performs a monthly bank reconciliation and maintains a manual purchase ledger control account.

Payroll

This is prepared by Susan using the computer.

There are 6 salaried staff including the directors, and 6 paid by the hour. They submit weekly time sheets which are signed as approved by the shop manager.

Saturday staff are paid in cash out of the till. All others are paid directly into their bank accounts.

The payroll is reviewed by Philip to identify any unusual amounts.

ANSWERS (Task 2)

Client	
Accounting date	

Prepared by	
Date	
Reviewed by	
Date	

_____

_____

_____

_____

_____

_____

_____

_____

_____

_____

_____

_____

_____

_____

_____

_____

_____

_____

_____

_____

_____

_____

_____

_____

_____

_____

ANSWERS (Task 2, continued)

Client	
Accounting date	

Prepared by	
Date	
Reviewed by	
Date	

ANSWERS (Task 2, continued)

Client	
Accounting date	

Prepared by	
Date	
Reviewed by	
Date	

_____

_____

_____

_____

_____

_____

_____

_____

_____

_____

_____

_____

_____

_____

_____

_____

_____

_____

_____

_____

_____

_____

_____

_____

_____

ANSWERS (Task 3)

Client	
Accounting date	

Prepared by	
Date	
Reviewed by	
Date	

ANSWERS (Task 4)

Client	
Accounting date	

Prepared by	
Date	
Reviewed by	
Date	

_____

_____

_____

_____

_____

_____

_____

_____

_____

_____

_____

_____

_____

_____

_____

_____

_____

_____

_____

_____

_____

_____

ANSWERS (Task 5)

Client	
Accounting date	

Prepared by	
Date	
Reviewed by	
Date	

ANSWERS (Task 5)

Client	
Accounting date	

Prepared by	
Date	
Reviewed by	
Date	

_____
_____
_____
_____
_____
_____
_____
_____
_____
_____
_____
_____
_____
_____
_____
_____
_____
_____
_____
_____
_____
_____
_____
_____
_____
_____
_____

ANSWERS (Task 6)

Client	
Accounting date	

Prepared by	
Date	
Reviewed by	
Date	

◇ **FOULKS**lynch

ANSWERS (Task 7)

MEMO

To:

From:

Date:

Subject: _____

_____

_____

_____

_____

_____

_____

_____

_____

_____

_____

_____

_____

_____

_____

_____

_____

_____

_____

_____

_____

_____

_____

_____

_____

_____

_____

_____

_____

ANSWERS (Task 7, continued)

ANSWERS (Task 8)

Client	ABC Ltd
Accounting date	30/09/97

Prepared by	JS
Date	x/x/9x
Reviewed by	
Date	

<u>Stock valuation test</u>

Selected at random

	Description	Quantity	Unit cost £	Total	Extension correct	Agreed to invoice	Net realisable value	Cost < NRV
1	Lge block Vanilla	30	0.75	22.50			2.00	
2	4 litr – Chocolate	110	6.30	693.00			12.00	
3	Mixed tubs	231	0.27	62.37			0.50	
4	Multi pack lollies	17	1.25	21.25			1.10	
5	Mars	58	0.40	23.20			0.60	
6	Twix	53	0.40	212.00			0.60	
7	Small cans	1,328	0.21	278.88			0.30	
8	Fiesta cone × 39	74	5.99	443.26			2.00	
9	Teddy bear cones	11	1.00	11.00			1.50	
10	Family pack flakes	27	0.78	21.06			1.00	
11	Sugar mice	57	0.20	11.40			0.40	
12	Carrier bags	900	17.10/1,000	15.39			–	
13	5 scoop pots and lids	1,250	0.13	162.50			0.25	
14	Opal fruits lollies	67	0.65	43.55			0.80	
15	Chocogrande	55	0.85	46.75			1.50	
16	Sunsational	64	0.31	19.84			0.75	
17	Yoghurt bars	79	19.76/pack	1,561.04			0.75	
18	Fudge bars	73	0.55	40.15			0.80	
19	Classic chocs	79	1.17	92.43			2.50	
20	White choc bars	72	0.50	36.00			1.00	

ANSWERS (Task 8, continued)

Client	
Accounting date	

Prepared by	
Date	
Reviewed by	
Date	

ANSWERS (Task 9)

Fixed assets – Depreciation calculation

Property – not depreciated

Fixtures and fittings – 20% reducing balance	
NBV b/f	62,500
Depreciation	(12,500)
NBV c/f	50,000

Equipment – 25% straight line	
NBV b/f	26,667
Depreciation	(6,667)
NBV c/f	20,000

Motor vehicles – 25% reducing balance	
NBV b/f	27,000
Additions	13,000
	40,000
Depreciation	(10,000)
NBV c/f	30,000

ANSWERS (Task 9, continued)

Client	
Accounting date	

Prepared by	
Date	
Reviewed by	
Date	

ANSWERS (Task 10)

Client	
Accounting date	

Prepared by	
Date	
Reviewed by	
Date	

_____

_____

_____

_____

_____

_____

_____

_____

_____

_____

_____

_____

_____

_____

_____

_____

_____

_____

_____

_____

_____

_____

_____

_____

_____

_____

ANSWERS (Task 10, continued)

Client	
Accounting date	

Prepared by	
Date	
Reviewed by	
Date	

ANSWERS (Task 11)

Client	ABC Ltd
Accounting date	30/09/97

Prepared by	JS
Date	x/x/9x
Reviewed by	
Date	

Purchases cut-off test

Objective – to ensure that purchases are recorded in the correct period.

Work done

5 deliveries before the year end and 5 after the year end were tested to ensure they were included in the purchase day book in the correct period.

Results

Deliveries pre year end

		£	
30/9/97	Simpson's Sweets	250	✓
30/9/97	Triangles and Treats	597	✓
30/9/97	Thornbury's	1,354	✗
30/9/97	Farthingales	50	✓
30/9/97	Sally Smiths	185	✓

ANSWERS (Task 11, continued)

Client	ABC Ltd
Accounting date	30/09/97

Prepared by	JS
Date	x/x/9x
Reviewed by	
Date	

Purchases cut-off – continued.

Deliveries post year end

		£	
1/10/97	Nice Ice Ltd	2,450	✓
1/10/97	Juicy Juices	1,751	✓
1/10/97	Barry's Business	600	✓
1/10/97	Lyons	50	✓
1/10/97	Alf's Afters	1,500	✓

Conclusion

ANSWERS (Task 12)

Client	
Accounting date	

Prepared by	
Date	
Reviewed by	
Date	

Management letter points

WEAKNESS	IMPLICATION	RECOMMENDATION

ANSWERS (Task 12, continued)

Client	
Accounting date	

Prepared by	
Date	
Reviewed by	
Date	

Management letter points – continued

WEAKNESS	IMPLICATION	RECOMMENDATION

◆ FOULKS*lynch*

ANSWERS (Task 13)

Client	
Accounting date	

Prepared by	
Date	
Reviewed by	
Date	

_____
_____
_____
_____
_____
_____
_____
_____
_____
_____
_____
_____
_____
_____
_____
_____
_____
_____
_____
_____
_____
_____
_____
_____
_____

If using this paper please indicate the task you are answering

Client	
Accounting date	

Prepared by	
Date	
Reviewed by	
Date	

_____

_____

_____

_____

_____

_____

_____

_____

_____

_____

_____

_____

_____

_____

_____

_____

_____

_____

_____

_____

_____

_____

_____

If using this paper please indicate the task you are answering

◈ FOULKS*lynch*

If using this paper please indicate the task you are answering

Client	
Accounting date	

Prepared by	
Date	
Reviewed by	
Date	

_____

_____

_____

_____

_____

_____

_____

_____

_____

_____

_____

_____

_____

_____

_____

_____

_____

_____

_____

_____

_____

_____

_____

_____

If using this paper please indicate the task you are answering

TECHNICIAN STAGE

NVQ/SVQ LEVEL 4 IN ACCOUNTING

AAT SPECIMEN SIMULATION

IMPLEMENTING AUDITING PROCEDURES

(UNIT 17)

ANSWERS (Task 1)

Client	ABC Ltd
Accounting date	30 September

Prepared by	AAS
Date	15/12/96
Reviewed by	AMM
Date	18/12/96

aat student x/x/9x

PERMANENT INFORMATION

HISTORY OF THE BUSINESS

ABC Ltd is a private limited company whose principal activity is the sale of ice cream and confectionery. It has been in operation for 10 years and runs four shops in the West of England within 30 miles of each other.

Shareholders – Philip Thompson (50%)
　　　　　　　Susan Thompson (50%) – Philip's wife

Directors – 　Philip Thompson
　　　　　　　Susan Thompson

Turnover is around £500,000 per shop with a net profit of £40,000 for the combined business.
One of the shops is owned by the company and valued at £150,000. The other premises are rented.

ACCOUNTING SYSTEMS

Computer environment
The computer uses Sage software. A hard copy is maintained of all entries into the computer. The password for access to the computer is known only to Philip and Susan. Whilst back up procedures are in place, Susan admits to forgetting to do this at times. There are no contingency plans should the computer fail.

Management accounts
Susan is responsible for the accounting function.

Monthly management accounts are produced by shop and by department (i.e. ice cream, chocolate, sweets, drinks). The system produces formatted Profit and Loss Account and Balance Sheet, detailed nominal ledger and aged creditors. Philip reviews the monthly management accounts.

ANSWERS (Task 1, continued)

Client	ABC Ltd
Accounting date	30 September

Prepared by	AAS
Date	15/12/96
Reviewed by	AMM
Date	18/12/96

aat student x/x/9x

Sales

All sales are cash sales. Cash is banked daily less incidental expenses and wages of Saturday staff. Invoices are kept for all incidental expenses. A reconciliation between the till roll and the cash in the till is performed daily by the manager of each shop.

Susan records sales from the till roll analysed between ice cream sales, and other sales and VAT.

Philip keeps a record of sales per staff hour in order to monitor the effectiveness of the staff.

Stock

The stock record is maintained on the computer. This is updated by Philip when a delivery is received, and updated automatically via the tills when a sale is made. Each shop performs a monthly stock check of a proportion of its stock to ensure that the computer figure is correct.

Stock is valued by the computer at the latest invoice prices.

ANSWERS (Task 1, continued)

Client	ABC Ltd
Accounting date	30 September

Prepared by	AAS
Date	15/12/96
Reviewed by	AMM
Date	18/12/96

aat student x/x/9x

Purchases and payments

Orders are made by Philip.

Deliveries are all made to Main Street, Taunton. Philip checks them against the order and delivery note and keeps the delivery note for agreement to the invoice; there is no evidence of Philip's check. He then delivers the goods to the other shops. This occurs once a week.

When the invoice arrives, Susan matches it to the delivery note and enters it on to the computer. The invoice and delivery note are stapled together for filing.

All other expenses are recorded on the computer when the invoice arrives.

Susan agrees the purchase ledger balance to the statements received each month.

All cheques are made out and signed by Susan. Philip is a cheque signatory but rarely gets involved with this.

Susan performs a monthly bank reconciliation and maintains a manual purchase ledger control account.

Payroll

This is prepared by Susan using the computer.

There are 6 salaried staff including the directors, and 6 paid by the hour. They submit weekly time sheets which are signed as approved by the shop manager.

Saturday staff are paid in cash out of the till. All others are paid directly into their bank accounts.

The payroll is reviewed by Philip to identify any unusual amounts.

ANSWERS (Task 2)

Client	ABC Ltd
Accounting date	30/9/97

Prepared by	AATS
Date	x/x/9x
Reviewed by	
Date	

INHERENT RISKS

Cash sales – possible understatement of sales.
Mis-statement of figures entered into till.
Error in input of stock to computer.
Error in inputting purchase invoices to computer.
Payroll hours incorrectly recorded.

CONTROLS

Close involvement of directors – controls all aspects of the business.
Well known and reliable software.
Maintenance of hard copy of all transactions.
Restricted knowledge of computer password.
Monthly management accounts reviewed by Philip – should pick up any unusual items.
Till reconciliation – confirms that the cash relating to the recorded sales has been put in the till.
Deliveries checked to purchase orders and delivery notes, and invoice matched to delivery note – ensures that payment is only made for goods that have been received.
Supplier statement reconciliation by Susan – confirms that creditors are correctly recorded.
Payroll hours approved by manager – prevents staff being paid for hours they have not worked.
Payment of wages into bank account – no risks of handling cash.
Payroll reviewed by Philip – any unusual amounts would be identified.
Bank reconciliation – ensures correct recording of payments and receipts.
Creditor's control account – ensures correct recording of purchases and payments (combined with supplier statement reconciliation).
Monthly stock check – confirms accuracy of stock records.
Sales per staff hour – keeps a check on the efficiency of staff, and would highlight excess hours. This is also a control over the sales figures as it could highlight inconsistencies in sales levels.

WEAKNESSES IN CONTROL

Irregular back up procedures.
No contingency plans should the computer fail.
Lack of segregation of duties, Susan is responsible for all of the accounting.
Cash is not banked intact, payments are made out of the till.
There is no batch control for the inputting of invoices into the computer.
There is no check that the price charged for purchases is correct.
Purchase invoices are not numbered on receipt.
Stock count is undertaken by staff who work in the shop.

ANSWERS (Task 3)

Client	ABC Ltd
Accounting date	30/9/97

Prepared by	AATS
Date	x/x/9x
Reviewed by	
Date	

TESTS OF CONTROL

Stock

Attend a monthly stock check at each shop to confirm the accuracy of the count and the computer record.

Purchases

The control whereby Philip agrees the delivery to the delivery note and the order can be tested by observation and enquiry. There is no other way to test this since Philip does not evidence his checks.

The control whereby Susan matches the delivery note to the invoice can be checked by observation and enquiry, and a sample can be tested to ensure invoices are attached to delivery notes.

ANSWERS (Task 4)

Client	ABC Ltd
Accounting date	30/9/97

Prepared by	AATS
Date	x/x/9x
Reviewed by	
Date	

The balances set out below should be audited on the basis that they are greater than materiality and there is potential for material error.   Prepayments and other creditors are excluded because they are below materiality and would be subject only to a review for reasonableness.

Fixed assets

To ensure that all assets owned by the company are recorded accurately at an appropriate value, and that depreciation has been correctly calculated.

Stock

To confirm that the quantity of stock is accurate, and that all stock owned by the company is included and only stock owned by the company is included. Also to ensure that stock is valued at the lower of cost and net realisable value.

Bank

To confirm that the amounts included in the figure for bank belong to the company and are accurately stated, and that all amounts have been included.

Trade creditors

To confirm that all liabilities are accurately recorded.

ANSWERS (Task 5)

Client	ABC Ltd
Accounting date	30/9/97

Prepared by	AATS
Date	x/x/9x
Reviewed by	
Date	

CREDITORS

The following creditors have been selected for testing on the basis that they are the largest creditors:

 Thornbury's
 Juicy Juices
 Nice Ice Ltd
 Alf's Afters
 Dairymen

(Alternative bases for selection are: systematic selection, random selection, judgmental selection – i.e. including a zero balance and a negative balance.)

The following work should be performed to confirm the accuracy of the balances:

 Agree to supplier's statement if available.
 Where no supplier's statement is available agree the build up of the balance to the invoices.

The following further work should be performed to confirm that all creditors are accurately recorded:

 Review invoices and payments recorded after the year end to identify any unrecorded liabilities.
 Enquire into Calvi's debit balance.
 Check the casting of the creditors' listing.
 Agree the total creditor figure to the purchase ledger control account.
 Confirm the constituent parts of the purchase ledger control account.
 Analytical procedures e.g. creditor days.

ANSWERS (Task 6)

Client	ABC Ltd
Accounting date	30/9/97

Prepared by	AATS
Date	x/x/9x
Reviewed by	
Date	

SALES

Tests for completeness and accuracy.

Analytical review:
- compare sales to the previous year on a monthly basis;
- review sales per staff hour to see if there is any suggestion of understatement;
- compare gross profit percentage with previous years, and with expectations.

Review till reconciliations for unexplained differences.

Test on a sample basis the posting from the till roll to the sales summary, and from the sales summary to the nominal ledger.

Ensure that the cut-off is correct, i.e. sales made in the last week of the year are included in the figures for the year.

PAYROLL

Tests for validity and accuracy.

Analytical review:
- compare the payroll with previous years on a monthly basis;
- review sales per staff hour to identify any potential incidences of overstatement of the payroll (in conjunction with above tests for sales);
- calculate the expected payroll by taking last year's payroll figure and adjusting it for changes in staff numbers and changes in rates of pay.

For staff paid by the hour agree a sample to time sheets, and agree rates of pay.

For salaried staff agree rates of pay.

Test calculations of rates of pay and deductions.

Confirm existence of staff.

ANSWERS (Task 7)

MEMO

To: Jo Smith

From: AAT Student

Date: x/x/9x

Subject: Audit sampling

Our manager has asked me to explain audit sampling to you. The principles are set out below, if you have any questions we can discuss them on Monday.

The purpose of sampling is to draw conclusions about the whole population on the basis of the sample.

There are various methods of selecting a sample, the most common are:

- random sampling where all items have an equal chance of being selected; the sample can be chosen using random number tables, or computer generated random numbers;

- systematic sampling – where items are selected at a constant interval from a random start. Different units of sampling may be used, i.e. invoice, balance, monetary unit;

- haphazard selection – any items are picked, but the auditor must be satisfied that the selection is not biased, and that the selection is made from a complete population.

If we find an error in a sample we should consider the nature, cause and possible effect of the error. We should project the error to consider the potential impact on the financial statements, and if this is likely to be material we should extend our audit procedures. All audit errors should be recorded on the unadjusted errors schedule.

Our manager has also asked me to explain your responsibilities regarding confidentiality and security.

Any information you obtain about this client during the audit should not be disclosed to any third party. Do not leave audit papers lying around for the client's staff to see, and if you take audit files home with you be very careful not to lose them and not to let any third party see them.

ANSWERS (Task 8)

Client	ABC Ltd
Accounting date	30/09/97

Prepared by	JS
Date	xx/xx/9x
Reviewed by	
Date	

Stock valuation test

Selected at random

	Description	Quantity	Unit cost £	Total	Extension correct	Agreed to invoice	Net realisable value	Cost < NRV
1	Lge block Vanilla	30	0.75	22.50	✓	✓	2.00	✓
2	4 litr – Chocolate	110	6.30	693.00	✓	✓	12.00	✓
3	Mixed tubs	231	0.27	62.37	✓	✓	0.50	✓
4	Multi pack lollies	17	1.25	21.25	✓	✓	1.10	✗
5	Mars	58	0.40	23.20	✓	✓	0.60	✓
6	Twix	53	0.40	212.00	✗	✓	0.60	✓
7	Small cans	1,328	0.21	278.88	✓	✓	0.30	✓
8	Fiesta cone × 39	74	5.99	443.26	✓	✗	2.00	✗
9	Teddy bear cones	11	1.00	11.00	✓	✓	1.50	✓
10	Family pack flakes	27	0.78	21.06	✓	✓	1.00	✓
11	Sugar mice	57	0.20	11.40	✓	✓	0.40	✓
12	Carrier bags	900	17.10/1,000	15.39	✓	✓	-	–
13	5 scoop pots and lids	1,250	0.13	162.50	✓	✓	0.25	✓
14	Opal fruits lollies	67	0.65	43.55	✓	✓	0.80	✓
15	Chocogrande	55	0.85	46.75	✓	✗	1.50	✓
16	Sunsational	64	0.31	19.84	✓	✗	0.75	✓
17	Yoghurt bars	79	19.76/pack	1,561.04	✗	✓	0.75	✗
18	Fudge bars	73	0.55	40.15	✓	✓	0.80	✓
19	Classic chocs	79	1.17	92.43	✓	✓	2.50	✓
20	White choc bars	72	0.50	36.00	✓	✓	1.00	✓

ANSWERS (Task 8, continued)

Client	ABC Ltd
Accounting date	30/09/97

Prepared by	AATS
Date	x/x/9x
Reviewed by	
Date	

Stock valuation test

Objective

To ensure that stock is valued at the lower of cost and net realisable value.

Work done

20 items were selected on a random basis. The extensions were checked, the cost was agreed to the latest invoice price, and the cost was compared with the net realisable value.

Results

The following errors were discovered:
The extension was incorrect for items 6 and 17.
The prices were incorrect for items 8, 15 and 16.
The net realisable value was less than cost for items 4, 8 and 17.

Conclusions

Due to the above errors it is not possible to conclude on the test at this stage.

Further work

Enquire into the reasons for the errors.
Project the errors.
Extend the tests if considered necessary.
Schedule the potential adjustments on the unadjusted errors schedule.

ANSWERS (Task 9)

ABC Ltd y/e 30/9/97

Fixed assets – Depreciation calculation

Property – not depreciated*	Received by AAT student – ×/×/9×

Fixtures and fittings – 20% reducing balance

NBV b/f	62,500
Depreciation	$(12,500)^c$
NBV c/f	50,000
	✓

Equipment – 25% straight line

NBV b/f	26,667
Depreciation	(6,667)*
NBV c/f	20,000
	✓

Motor vehicles – 25% reducing balance

NBV b/f	27,000
Additions	13,000*
	40,000
Depreciation	$(10,000)^c$
NBV c/f	30,000
	✓

<u>Code</u>
^{c} = Calculation correct
✓ = cast correct
* see next page

ANSWERS (Task 9, continued)

Client	ABC Ltd
Accounting date	30/09/97

Prepared by	AATS
Date	x/x/9x
Reviewed by	
Date	

Fixed assets – errors

Non depreciation of property does not comply with FRS 15. However, if this is justifiable, disclosure of non-compliance will suffice.

The depreciation of equipment has been calculated on the reducing balance basis instead of the straight line basis.

The cost used for the vehicle is the net figure. It should be the VAT inclusive figure.

ANSWERS (Task 10)

Client	**ABC Ltd**
Accounting date	*30/09/97*

Prepared by	**AATS**
Date	*xx/xx/9x*
Reviewed by	
Date	

Suppliers' statements reconciliation

Objective

To ensure all creditors are correctly recorded.

Work done

A sample of 5 creditors were agreed or reconciled to the supplier's statement.

Results

	Balance per ABC Ltd	Balance per statement	Reconciling items	Agreed/ reconciled
Thornbury's	19,123	20,477	£1,354 – invoice on statement not on ledger.	✓
Juicy Juices	17,214	18,214	£1,000 paid – on ledger not on statement	✓
Nice Ice Ltd	19,111	19,111	–	✓
Alf's Afters	17,283	17,283	–	✓
Dairymen	12,480	14,460	£1,980 – invoice on statement not on ledger.	✓

Conclusion

The invoices from Thornbury's and Dairymen should be included in purchases and creditors provided they relate to goods received before the year end. The potential adjustment is:

    Debit purchases   3,334
        Credit creditors   3,334

The above suggest cut-off errors, and the purchases cut-off testing should be extended to ensure no further errors.

ANSWERS (Task 11)

Client	ABC Ltd
Accounting date	*30/09/97*

Prepared by	JS
Date	*xx/xx/9x*
Reviewed by	
Date	

Purchases cut-off test

Objective – to ensure that purchases are recorded in the correct period.

Work done

5 deliveries before the year end and 5 after the year end were tested to ensure they were included in the purchase day book in the correct period.

Results

Deliveries pre year end

		£	Included in correct period
30/9/97	*Simpson's Sweets*	*250*	✓
30/9/97	*Triangles and Treats*	*597*	✓
30/9/97	*Thornbury's*	*1,354*	✗
30/9/97	*Farthingales*	*50*	✓
30/9/97	*Sally Smiths*	*185*	✓

ANSWERS (Task 11, continued)

Client	ABC Ltd
Accounting date	*30/09/97*

Prepared by	JS
Date	*x/x/9x*
Reviewed by	
Date	

Purchases cut-off – continued.

Deliveries post year end

		£	Included in correct period
1/10/97	*Nice Ice Ltd*	*2,450*	✓
1/10/97	*Juicy Juices*	*1,751*	✓
1/10/97	*Barry's Business*	*600*	✓
1/10/97	*Lyons*	*50*	✓
1/10/97	*Alf's Afters*	*1,500*	✓

Conclusion
The late posting of the Thornbury's invoice suggests that there may be further cut-off errors. The test for pre year end deliveries should be extended unless an explanation is obtained for the late posting which satisfies us that it is an isolated incident. See also the results of the suppliers' statements reconciliation.

ANSWERS (Task 12)

Client	ABC Ltd
Accounting date	30/9/97

Prepared by	AATS
Date	×/×/9×
Reviewed by	
Date	

Management letter points*

WEAKNESS	IMPLICATION	RECOMMENDATION
Inconsistent back up procedures.	Loss of data should computer fail.	Back up after every batch input.
No contingency plans should computer fail.	If the computer fails, there could be problems in keeping accounting records up to date.	Arrange for alternative computer facilities which could be used in the event of a computer breakdown.
Lack of segregation of duties, especially in respect of cheque payments.	Errors or misappropriations may go undetected.	Philip should review cheque payments before they are made.
Cash from the till is not banked intact.	There is scope for cash to go missing.	A separate petty cash system should be maintained.
Inputting of invoice onto computer with no control.	An invoice could be missed, or incorrectly entered. The control account reconciliation would not pick this up.	Manual totalling of batches of invoices before entry, and following entry confirm that the batch agrees to the manual total.
No check that the price charged for purchases is correct.	Overpayment for purchases. Incorrect valuation of stock	The price should be checked to the price list or quote before input into the computer.
Purchase invoices are not numbered upon receipt.	Purchase invoices may go missing and therefore not be recorded.	Number purchase invoices sequentially upon receipt.
Stock count is performed by staff who work in the shop.	Staff may miscount to cover their own errors or misappropriations	Stock should be counted by staff from different shops.

Please see pages 69 - 70 for assessment criteria. Only two points need to be included.

ANSWERS (Task 13)

Client	ABC Ltd
Accounting date	30/9/97

Prepared by	AATS
Date	×/×/9×
Reviewed by	
Date	

AUDITORS' REPORT TO THE SHAREHOLDERS OF
ABC LIMITED FOR THE YEAR ENDED 30 SEPTEMBER 1997

OPINION

In our opinion the financial statements give a true and fair view of the state of the company's affairs as at 30 September 1997 and of its profit for the year then ended, and have been properly prepared in accordance with the Companies Act 1985 applicable to small companies.

COVERAGE OF PERFORMANCE CRITERIA

The following performance criteria are covered in this simulation. An indication of which performance criteria are covered by the individual tasks is given in brackets following the task assessment criteria (see pages 69 – 70).

Element	PC Coverage
17.1 (i) (ii) (iii) (iv) (v) (vi) (vii) (viii) (ix)	**Contribute to the planning of an audit assignment.** • Systems under review are ascertained and clearly recorded on appropriate working papers. • Control objectives are correctly identified. • Risks are accurately assessed. • Significant weaknesses in control are correctly recorded. • Account balances to be verified and the associated risks are identified. • An appropriate sample is selected. • Appropriate tests are selected or devised in accordance with the organisation's procedures. • Confidentiality and security procedures are followed. • The proposed audit plan is formulated clearly in consultation with appropriate personnel and submitted for approval to the appropriate person.
17.2 (i) (ii) (iii) (iv) (v) (vii)	**Contribute to the conduct of an audit assignment.** • Tests, as specified in the audit plan, are correctly conducted, the results properly recorded and conclusions validly drawn. • The existence, completeness, ownership, valuation and description of assets and liabilities is established and supported by appropriate evidence. • All matters of an unusual nature are identified and promptly referred to the audit supervisor. • Material and significant errors, deficiencies or other variations from standard are identified, recorded and reported to the audit supervisor. • The IT environment is examined and assessed for security. • Confidentiality and security procedures are followed.
17.3 (i) (ii) (iii) (iv) (v)	**Prepare related draft reports.** • Clear, concise draft reports relating to the audit assignment are prepared and submitted for review and approval in accordance with organisational procedures. • Conclusions are valid and supported by evidence. • Recommendations are constructive and practicable. • Preliminary conclusions and recommendations are discussed and agreed with the audit supervisor. • Confidentiality and security procedures are followed.

The following performance criterion from element 17.2 (17.2 (vi)) is not covered in this simulation and should be separately assessed:
• Discussions with staff operating the system to be audited are conducted in a manner which promotes professional relationships between auditing and operational staff.

ASSESSMENT CRITERIA

Auditing is a matter of professional opinion and subjective judgement and it is therefore inappropriate to be too rigid in the answers to be given to this simulation. However, in all cases the objective of the task must be achieved, and any justification given must be assessed for its reasonableness; the work done must be in accordance with that justification.

(Task 1 – 6 together cover performance criteria 17.1 (i) – (ix))

TASK 1
The systems notes should be updated so that they correctly reflect the changes to the systems. Omission of the signing and dating of the schedule is permitted. (17.1 (i))

TASK 2
Omission of 2 risks, 4 controls, and 2 weaknesses in control is permitted. Incorrect identification of risks, controls and weaknesses constitutes an error; no such error is permitted. It is essential that the risks, controls and weaknesses identified relate to the system under review. (17.1(i), (ii), (iii), (iv) and 17.2 (v))

TASK 3
Any tests suggested which will confirm the operation of the control are acceptable. Tests suggested which do not do this constitute an error; one such error is permitted. (17.1 (vii))

TASK 4
The justification is key to this task. Any reasonable justification is permissible; the balances selected for testing must accord with the justification. No omission is permitted in the audit objectives. (17.1 (v))

TASK 5
Any 5 balances may be selected as long as the justification is reasonable, and the selection is in accordance with the justification.

The tests suggested must include:
* suppliers' statement test;
* post year end review;
* enquiry into the debit balance.

Tests suggested which do not achieve the objectives constitute an error. One such error is permitted. (17.1 (vii))

TASK 6
Any tests which fully achieve the objectives are acceptable. A test which does not achieve the objectives constitutes an error. One such error is permitted. (17.1 (vii))

TASK 7
Correct explanation of the purpose of sampling must be provided.
At least two methods of selecting a sample must be given.
Dealing with errors must include projection of the error, and the possibility of extending the tests.
It must be made clear that all information is confidential. (17.1 (vi), (viii), 17.2 (vii), 17.3 (v))

TASK 8
The working paper must be properly headed and should clearly state the objective, the work done, the results and conclusion.
All errors must be identified.
Suggestions for further work may omit the point to schedule potential adjustments.
The test schedule must be properly completed. (17.2 (i), (ii), (iii), (iv))

TASK 9

The schedule should be properly annotated to show the work done. All errors must be identified. (17.2 (i), (ii), (iii), (iv))

TASK 10

The working paper must be properly headed up and set out objectives, work done, results and conclusions. All balances must be properly reconciled, and the problems correctly identified. No omissions are permitted. (17.2(i), (ii), (iii), (iv))

TASK 11

The conclusion including any further action to be taken, must be correct. (17.2 (i), (iii), (iv))

TASK 12

Two weaknesses must be included, and they must relate to ABC Ltd. Implications must be correctly identified, and practical and appropriate recommendations must be given. (17.3 (i), (ii), (iii), (iv))

TASK 13

The paragraph does not need to be word perfect, but reference must be made to:
- true and fair view;
- year end;
- properly prepared in accordance with the Companies Act 1985. (17.3 (i), (ii))

OVERALL ASSESSMENT

General
- It is expected that work will be neatly and competently presented
- Pencil is not acceptable
- Liquid correcting fluid may be used but it should be used in moderation.

Discretion

In having regard to the above criteria, the assessor is entitled in marginal cases to exercise discretion in the candidate's favour. Such discretion shall only be exercised where other criteria are met to above the required standard and, in the opinion of the assessor, the assessment overall demonstrates competence and would be of an acceptable standard in the workplace.

QUESTIONS

Chapters 1-2

FRAMEWORK OF AUDITING

---

1 Activity

You are an audit senior in a firm of accountants who has been invited to tender for the audit of a medium sized manufacturing company Foodies Ltd.

Foodies Ltd is a private limited company and has 200 employees including 3 directors. They incorporated 10 years ago and their profits have been increasing steadily since then. Their current auditors have decided to resign as they do not consider they have sufficient staff to be able to satisfactorily perform the work.

Task

One of the partners of your firm has asked you to prepare a working paper for him providing him with details of the factors that should be considered by your firm in deciding whether or not to bid for the audit.

---

2 Activity

Foodies Ltd have selected your firm as their auditors. A planning meeting has been scheduled with the Audit Partner in charge and the Audit Manager to discuss the audit approach.

Task

Prepare a working paper which will form part of the agenda for the meeting outlining four matters that will require particular attention during your firm's first audit of Foodies Ltd, as their year end is fast approaching (30 November).

Chapters 3-4

COMPANIES ACTS REQUIREMENTS

1   Activity

You have just qualified as an Accounting Technician and have decided to study for a professional accountancy qualification which your firm has offered to sponsor you for.

They have also decided to employ two junior members of staff to study for their AAT qualification and have asked you to spend some time with them explaining exactly what is required of them as accountants by law and by the Association of Accounting Technicians.

Task 1

Prepare a memorandum addressed to the partners of the firm outlining the provisions of the CA85 which strengthen the independence of the auditor.

This will then be reviewed by the partners prior to being given to the junior members of staff.

Task 2

Explain to the junior auditors the requirements of the AAT's Professional Conduct Rule on Integrity, Objectivity and Independence which strengthen the independence of the auditor.

Chapter 5

AUDIT APPOINTMENT

1	Activity

You are the audit senior in a firm who has recently completed the audit of Bentfasteners Ltd, and after extensive discussions with the directors of the company, the audit report has been qualified in respect of the auditors' inability to agree with the directors on the appropriateness of a provision against obsolete stock. The directors have informed you that they intend to dismiss your firm as auditors, and replace you with a small local firm of accountants. The directors have informed you verbally that the reason for your dismissal is the disagreement over the provision for stock obsolescence, and further they intend to appoint the new auditors because they are more likely to accept the accounting policies of the directors. Your firm has recently received a letter from the nominee auditors asking if there are any professional reasons why they should not accept appointment as auditors of Bentfasteners Ltd.

Task 1

Prepare a working paper for the audit partners to be used in a meeting to discuss the current situation with Bentfasteners. The working paper should outline the rights which the CA85 gives to the auditor when a company proposes to dismiss him and has dismissed him.

Task 2

Draft a suitable letter in reply to the request from the nominee firm of auditors asking if there are any reasons why they should not accept appointment as auditors.

Task 3

One of the junior auditors who has just commenced employment with the firm is very interested in the situation and would like to discuss it with you further; he asks you to explain what the ethical implications for the nominee auditor are if he decides to accept appointment as auditor.

Draft a suitable response (in memorandum form) to the junior auditor.

Chapter 6

PLANNING THE AUDIT

---

1 Activity

You are the manager responsible for the audit of Williams Ltd, a company which manufactures magnetic media products.

You are planning the audit for the year ending 30 June 20X2. From your discussions with the finance director, you ascertain that during the year the company made a significant investment in equipment comprising a moulding machine and a conveyor system which have been included in the fixed asset register at £525,000.

The moulding machine is used to produce floppy disks and the conveyor system carries the disks from production to the packing department. The moulding machine was purchased on 1 March 20X2 from the manufacturer in Germany and the price was agreed in Deutschmarks, payable one half on 1 March 20X2 and the balance 60 days later.

The conveyor system was designed and constructed by the company's employees using components specifically bought in.

You also ascertain that the company's application for a Government grant of £95,000 in respect of other fixed assets, acquired earlier in the year, has been submitted and approved. The expenditure relating to these fixed assets has already been verified as the company's grant application was reported on by your firm. However the company had not received the grant at the time of your discussions with the finance director.

Task

You are required to prepare, for inclusion in an audit planning memorandum, a list of the potential risks of misstatement in respect of the above items and the steps that you would take to address them.

---

2 Activity

Gower Ltd buys in coal which is washed and sorted into different grades prior to selling to commercial and domestic customers. Coal is purchased from local mines and also imported from the Far East. Imports are landed at a nearby port, stored there and transported to a company's premises only when there is sufficient storage capacity.

The company does not maintain continuous stock records. Purchases are recorded in a goods received book and sales are recorded on sequentially numbered despatch notes. All stock movements are checked on the weighbridge.

The company also washes and sorts coal for other merchants. Each merchant is charged a fee, by Gower Ltd, per ton of coal washed and sorted.

Stock quantities are ascertained for the annual financial statements by a physical count. This is conducted by an independent quantity surveyor who calculates the volume of stock and subsequently converts the results for each grade into tonnage.

You are the auditor of Gower Ltd and last year you included an explanatory paragraph in the audit report due to uncertainty over the stock figure. This was because, subsequent to the count, it came to light that different grades of coal had been mixed accidentally and the quantity surveyor had treated them as one grade.

The managing director has informed you that the stocktake will be held at the year end which will be a Saturday. Business will continue as usual until lunchtime. The stocktake will last all day.

Due to the problems last year you intend to consider carefully the arrangements for the stocktake.

Task 1

Prepare, for inclusion in a planning memorandum, a list of potential audit risks in respect of the ascertainment of stock quantities and the steps that you would take to address them.

Task 2

Explain why it is important for you to attend the stocktake even though a specialist is used to quantify the stock.

Chapters 7-8

INTERNAL CONTROLS AND AUDIT TESTING

1	Activity

Burnden Ltd manufactures a range of components and spare parts for the textile industry. The company employs 150 hourly-paid production workers and 20 administrative staff, including the three directors of the company. There are two wages clerks who deal with the weekly payroll of the hourly-paid employees. They are directly responsible to the assistant accountant.

The company uses a computerised time clock at the factory gate to record the hours worked by the production employees. Each employee has a card with a magnetic strip with his own identification code on it. This card is inserted in the computerised time clock on the arrival and departure of the workers, whereupon it records the hours worked on the card. The cards are collected weekly by the wages clerks, who simply insert them individually into the microcomputer, which then reads them and prepares the payroll. The production manager keeps the unused clock cards in a locked cabinet in his office.

Wages are paid one week in arrears. The wages clerks compile the payroll by means of the microcomputer system, pass the payroll to the assistant accountant who scrutinises it before drawing the wages cheque, which is passed to one of the directors for signature. Any pay increases are negotiated locally by representatives of the employees. If any alterations are required to the standing data on the microcomputer, then the wages clerks amend the records. For example, when a wage increase has been negotiated, the rates of pay are changed by the wages clerks.

The cheque is drawn to cover net wages and the cashier makes arrangements for collecting the cash from the bank. The wages clerks then make up the wages envelopes. Whenever there is assistance required on preparing wages, the assistant accountant helps the wages clerks. The payment of wages is carried out by the production manager who returns any unclaimed wages to the wages clerks who keep them in a locked filing cabinet. Each employee is expected to collect his unclaimed wages personally.

New production employees are notified to the wages department verbally by the production manager and when employees leave, a note to that effect is sent to the wages department by the production manager. All statutory deductions are paid to the appropriate authorities by the chief accountant.

Administrative staff are paid monthly by credit transfer to their bank account. The payroll is prepared by the assistant accountant and the bank credit transfers are authorised by a director. Any increases in the salaries of the administrative staff are notified to the assistant accountant verbally by the chief accountant. The employment of administrative staff is authorised by the financial director.

You have recently been appointed the auditor of Burnden Ltd for the year ended 31 December 20X8 and have just started your interim audit. You are about to commence your audit evaluation and testing of the wages system.

Task 1

Prepare a schedule which details the weaknesses in the present wages and salaries system, the possible effect of such weaknesses, and suggest, with reasons, improvements which could be made to the system (assuming that the only controls are those set out above).

Task 2

Prepare audit programmes detailing the audit tests required to ensure that the wages and salaries are completely and accurately recorded. (Note: tests of control and substantive tests should be shown on different audit programmes).

---

2   Activity

The Midas Mail Order Company operates a central warehouse from which all merchandise is distributed by post or carrier to the company's 10,000 customers. An outline description of the sales and cash collection system is set out below; this forms part of the systems documentation in the audit file.

Sales and cash collection system

Stage	Department/staff responsible	Documentation
Customer orders merchandise	Sales department Sales assistants	Multiple copy order form (with date, quantities, price marked on them).
Orders by telephone or through the postal system		Copies 1-3 sent to warehouse. Copy 4 sent to accounts department. Copy 5 retained in sales department.
Merchandise requested from stock rooms by despatch clerks	Secure stockrooms. Storekeepers	Copies 1-3 handed to storekeepers. Forms marked as merchandise taken from stock. (Note if merchandise is out of stock, the storekeepers retain Copies 1-3 until stockroom is restocked.) Copies 1-2 handed to despatch clerks.
Merchandise despatched	Despatch bay Despatch clerks	Copy 1 sent with merchandise as despatch note.
Customers invoiced	Accounts department Sales ledger clerks	2-copy invoice prepared from details on Copy 2 of order form received from despatch bay. Copy 1 sent to customer. Copy 2 retained by accounts department and posted to sales ledger.
Cash received (as cheques, bank giro credit or cash)	Accounts department Cashier	2-copy cash receipt list. Copy 1 retained by cashier. Copy 2 passed to sales ledger clerk.

You are a member of the audit team about to commence the testing stage of the audit (financial year ended 31/12/X7) and have been assigned the task of completing the testing for the Sales and Cash Collection system.

Task 1

Prepare an audit programme detailing the tests of control you would perform to test the controls in the Sales and Cash Collection system.

Task 2

State four objectives of an internal control system.

---

3   Activity

Your firm has been appointed auditor of Wicket Ltd, a company which manufactures furniture. The company employs sixty weekly-paid employees comprising upholsterers, carpenters, joiners and general labourers. All employees are paid by credit transfer directly into their bank accounts.

The payroll is processed using a microcomputer with a hard disk which stores the payroll program, standing and transactions data relating to employees. On completion of payroll processing, the hard disk is copied onto a floppy disk which is stored in one of the filing cabinets in the accounts office.

Hours worked are recorded on clock cards. Employees clock in and out on arrival at and departure from the premises. At the end of each week, the factory manager, Mr Lamb, gives the accounts supervisor, Mrs Gooch, the clock cards for that week and collects the clock cards for the following week. Each employee's name and number is entered on the card by Mrs Gooch.

Mrs Gooch calculates for each employee the hours worked, split between basic and overtime. The cards are then passed to Miss Smith, the payroll clerk, who enters the details into the computer. The figures for gross and net pay are calculated by the program and the following reports are generated:

Payroll:	details per employee of gross pay, deductions and net pay; totals thereof and total hours split between basic and overtime;
Summary:	cumulative details to date per employee;
Payslips:	details of gross pay, deductions and net pay;
Giro list:	bank account details, net pay per employee and total net pay.

The finance director, Mr Lewis, signs the cheque after agreeing it to the total net pay on the giro list and passes the cheque to the managing director, Mr Stewart, who countersigns it.

Mr Lamb gives a list detailing starters and leavers to Miss Smith who enters these changes into the computer as and when the situation arises. She uses the same password as for payroll preparation even though there is a facility within the software for hierarchical passwords. Miss Smith then files the list with the personnel records in her filing cabinet.

Your enquiries about the system indicate that there are no relevant procedures or controls other than those described above.

Task

Prepare a weakness schedule which documents the weaknesses in the wages system, together with associated effects and your recommendations.

4   Activity

The managing director of H plc read a newspaper report of a fraud which had recently come to the attention of the police. The perpetrators had sent invoices to several thousand companies. These requested payment for an entry in a trade directory.

The directory did not, however, exist. The newspaper report claimed that approximately 700 companies had paid £2,000 each for an entry in this alleged directory. H plc's managing director asked whether the company had received one of these invoices. It was discovered that H plc was one of the companies which had paid the £2,000 charge. The reason for this payment was investigated.

H plc's accounting system was recently computerised. All invoices are keyed straight into a standard accounting package. The company's accounting department is short staffed and so the default settings on the package have been set to minimise the amount of clerical effort required to process transactions. If, for example, an invoice is received from a new supplier, the program will automatically allocate an account number and open an account in the purchase ledger. At the end of every month, the program calculates the amount which is due to each creditor; a cheque for each creditor is automatically printed out for the total of all of the invoices from that creditor input during the month. When the system was first installed, the accountant used to review creditors' accounts prior to the cheque run as a check that the system was not being abused. This review was, however, discontinued because of pressure of work and because there were too many invoices to review properly.

The managing director was most disturbed by this description of the purchases system and decided that it was in urgent need of improvement. The company's accountant was ordered to redesign the system. The accountant was authorised to employ additional staff if the extra expense could be justified.

Task

Prepare a weakness schedule describing three weaknesses which exist in H plc's purchasing system, the effects/implications of those weaknesses, and make recommendations for their improvements.

Chapter 9
SAMPLING

1	Activity

Cromwell Ltd sells fashion accessories through approximately 500 shops and has a head office in Andover.

Each shop operates an imprest system and holds a cash float of £250 to provide change for the till and to cover sundry expenses. All cash takings are banked at the end of each working day.

You are the senior in charge of the audit and your manager has indicated that only a sample of the cash balances held by the shops will be the subject of audit tests.

Many of the fashion accessories are purchased from foreign suppliers and the company's buyers frequently travel abroad. The cashier at head office therefore holds a substantial amount of foreign currency in her safe.

The company has recently expanded its accessory range and just prior to year end received a bank loan of £100,000 repayable over 3 years.

The cash balance at year end 31 March 20X7 totalled £100,000.

Task 1

Prepare an audit programme detailing the tests you would perform to verify the following figures in the balance sheet:

- Cash balance
- Bank loan

Task 2

Prepare a 'general' working paper explaining the main factors which will be taken into account when determining the sample size for substantive testing. This will be used to assist the other members of the audit team helping you with the testing.

Chapters 10-12

AUDIT OF STOCKS AND FIXED ASSETS

1 Activity

You are the audit senior working on the audit of Northern Supplies plc, and are just about to commence the testing to verify the balance in the accounts for fixed assets.

During the year to 28 February 20X7 Northern Supplies plc has acquired a new computer which, although it cost less than the previous machine, is more powerful. The company has transferred its existing systems on to the new computer system during the year, and disposed of its old computer. It now proposes to transfer its fixed assets register which previously was handwritten, to the new computer with effect from 28 February 20X7. The company proposes to develop its own software to deal with the new application.

Task 1

Prepare an audit programme detailing the tests to be performed to verify the figures in the financial statements as at 28 February 20X7 for the purchase of the new computer and the sale of the existing computer.

Task 2

Write a memorandum to the Audit Manager stating the problems you think you may encounter when deciding whether or not the new computer is properly stated in the fixed assets figure.

2 Activity

You are the audit manager in charge of the audit of Camry Products Ltd; the remainder of the audit team comprise an audit senior and 3 audit juniors. Although the audit juniors have been with the firm for 8 months they have never attended a stocktake and you consider that this will be useful and beneficial to them. The audit senior has only attended one stocktake previously.

You have called a meeting with the audit team to give them some guidance and advice on the work to be performed. The audit senior has provided you with the following information in respect of the procedures performed by Camry Products.

Camry Products Ltd's, financial year end is 31 March 20X9 and they intend to perform a physical stock count at their warehouse at this date. The company assembles domestic appliances, and stocks of finished appliances, unassembled parts and sundry stocks are stored in the warehouse which is adjacent to the company's assembly plant. The plant will continue to produce goods during the stock count until 5 pm on 31 March 20X9. On 30 March 20X9, the warehouse staff will deliver the estimated quantities of unassembled parts and sundry stocks which will be required for production for 31 March 20X9; however, emergency requisitions by the factory will be filled on 31 March. During the stock count, the warehouse staff will continue to receive parts and sundry stocks, and to despatch finished appliances. Appliances which are completed on 31 March 20X9 will remain in the assembly plant until after the physical stock count has been completed.

Task 1

Prepare a working paper for use at the meeting indicating the procedures that the auditor should perform when planning his attendance at the stocktake.

Task 2

The audit senior has been suddenly taken ill, and did not have time to complete the audit programme to test the accuracy of stock cut off. In order to prevent any delay to the timetable you are required to undertake this task. Prepare an audit programme identifying the audit tests that you would carry out for this purpose.

Task 3

The Stores Manager, Mr. Biggs has approached you and asked for some advice on the procedures they should perform to ensure that they only count stock items once. Write a letter to Mr Biggs detailing the methods that he should adopt and explaining why such procedures are important to Camry Products Ltd.

---

3   Activity

Your firm is the auditor of Barnes Wholesalers Limited, and as audit senior you have been asked to carry out audit checks on cut-off and verifying stock quantities at the year-end.

The company maintains details of stock quantities on its computer. These stock quantities are updated from goods received notes, and sales invoices. The company carries out stocktakes each month, when all the fast moving and high value stock is counted, and a third of the remaining stock is counted in rotation so that all stock items are counted at least four times a year.

You attend the stocktake on Sunday 13 October, and a further stocktake was carried out on Sunday 10 November. The company's year-end was Thursday 31 October 20X8 and the stock quantities at that date, as shown by the computer, have been used in the valuation of the stock. No stock was counted at the year-end.

Extracts from the stock records system are shown below:

Extract from stock records system / stock count records

Goods Despatched Notes Log		Goods Received Notes Log	
Date	**No.**	**Date**	**No.**
6/4/X8	307	1/4/X8	899
18/4/X8	308	6/5/X8	900
3/5/X8	309	17/6/X8	901
25/5/X8	310	3/7/X8	902
27/5/X8	311	19/8/X8	903
1/6/X8	312	26/9/X8	904
2/7/X8	313	3/10/X8	905
7/7/X8	314	1/11/X8	906
11/7/X8	315	9/12/X8	907
15/7/X8	316	16/1/X9	908
21/7/X8	317	5/2/X9	909

Goods despatched Notes Log		Goods received Notes Log	
Date	**No.**	**Date**	**No.**
4/8/X8	318		
17/8/X8	319		
6/9/X8	320		
21/9/X8	321		
3/10/X8	322		
17/10/X8	323		
1/11/X8	324		
3/11/X8	325		
6/12/X8	326		
21/12/X8	327		
3/1/X9	328		
16/1/X9	329		
18/2/X9	330		
19/2/X9	331		

- There were 100 stock sheets used in the stocktake as a separate one was used for each product. These were sequentially numbered 1-100.

- Separate caged areas were used to hold any stock that was delivered during the stocktake.

- During the stocktake it was noted that there were ten stock items where there had been no movement in the last year.

Task 1

Prepare an audit programme detailing the tests you would perform to check that sales and purchases cut off have been correctly carried out at both the date of the stocktake and at the year end.

Task 2

Following your attendance at the stocktake on 13 October, write up your working papers stating the principal matters which you checked (ie, typical checks that the auditor would perform) and clearly show the data you recorded (using the extract from the stock records system and stock count).

Task 3

Prepare an audit programme detailing the tests you would perform to satisfy yourself that the stock quantities used in the end of year stock valuation are correct.

---

4   Activity

Your firm has recently been appointed auditor of Andrew Manufacturing Limited, and you have been asked to carry out the audit of fixed assets at the company's year-end of 30 September 20X4.

The company operates from its own freehold premises, and the draft accounts show the following movement on fixed assets for the year.

	Freehold land and buildings £	Plant and machinery £	Motor vehicles £	Total £
Cost:				
At 1 October 20X3	162,577	46,003	20,175	229,295
Additions	2,534	8,721	7,500	18,755
Disposals	-	(5,937)	(5,250)	(11,187)
At 30 September 20X4	165,111	48,787	22,965	236,863
Depreciation:				
At 1 October 20X3	2,104	20,059	10,353	32,516
Charge for the year	1,102	4,878	5,741	11,721
On disposals	-	(4,808)	(3,937)	(8,745)
At 30 September 20X4	3,206	20,129	12,157	35,492

It is the company's policy to charge a full year's depreciation in the year of acquisition and nothing in the year of disposal.

The company's accounting policies are to provide depreciation at the following rates:

Buildings	4% on cost
Plant and machinery	10% on cost
Motor vehicles	25% on cost

The company maintains a fixed asset register for plant and machinery and motor vehicles.

Task 1

Prepare an audit programme detailing the tests you would perform for the audit of fixed assets for the year ended 30/9/X4.

Task 2

As Audit Senior prepare a memorandum to the junior auditor assisting you on the audit explaining why the fixed asset register is such an important control and highlight the problems that would be caused if it did not exist.

Chapter 13

AUDIT OF DEBTORS AND CASH

1	Activity

You are a senior audit clerk and are briefing an experienced junior auditor who is about to commence the audit of the debtors of Askwith Ltd. The sales ledger is maintained by the client on a mainframe computer. Sales invoice and credit note data are fed to the computer via 12 terminals in regional offices. All cash entries, journal entries relating to bad debts and other adjustments, and any other special entries are input via two terminals located at the client's head office. The computer produces, as a monthly routine, an aged debtors' schedule containing on average 3,000 live balances. You tell the junior auditor to verify the accuracy of the aged debtors' schedule including arranging for circulars to be sent to a representative sample of debtors. To assist the junior in this task you provide him with a copy of the audit programme.

The audit programme contains, among other things, the following:

(a) For balances over £1,000 at the year-end, use special computer audit program to dump transaction details for one month prior to the year-end and for one month after the year-end.

(b) Circularise debtors (seeking a positive response) and follow up those who do not reply.

(c) Test cut-off using dumped transactions.

The new junior audit clerk is still a little confused by some of the terminology being used, the reasons underlying your requests and the detail of the techniques being used, and has asked you for further assistance and information.

Task 1

Draft a suitable letter to be used to circularise the debtors.

Task 2

Explain to the junior auditor the steps that should be taken if no reply is received from the debtors and explain what alternative procedures might be used to verify the balances.

Task 3

Prepare an audit programme for the audit of the financial statements for the year ended 30/6/X8 detailing the cut off tests that should be used to verify that the cut off for debtors is correct.

Chapter 14

AUDIT OF LIABILITIES

1	Activity

You are the manager in charge of the audit of Farrington Ltd, a company which manufactures biscuits and confectionery. You wish to instruct a junior member of staff to audit the trade creditors, accruals and provisions as shown in the balance sheet at the year-end and are in the process of preparing audit programmes which clearly explain the purpose and extent of the work at each stage of the audit.

The draft figures for 'creditors - amounts falling due within one year' as at 31 October 20X5 (with 20X4 comparative figures) are as follows:

	31 October	
	20X5	*20X4*
	£	£
Trade creditors	261,521	177,625
Sundry accruals	21,162	18,177
Provisions:		
Legal action*	40,000	-
Factory repairs**	72,000	62,000
	394,683	257,802

*   This provision relates to a legal action brought by a competitor who claims that their manufacturing process has been illegally copied.

**   This provision, which was first set up in 20X4, relates to sums required to be spent on urgent repairs to the factory foundations and structural steelwork. (£58,500 was spent during the year ended 31 October 20X5).

Task 1

Prepare an audit programme detailing the tests to be performed to verify the figure for Trade Creditors.

Task 2

Prepare an audit programme detailing the tests to be performed to verify the figure for Sundry Accruals.

Task 3

Prepare an audit programme detailing the tests to be performed to verify the figure for Provisions.

Chapter 15

COMPUTERS IN AUDIT

---

1   Activity

Kola Ltd is a wholesaler of toys and novelty goods. The directors, and major shareholders, are Tom and Fred Simms.

The company sells to both large and small retailers. It has approximately 750 active customers on its sales ledger and stocks a very wide range of items. It has recently purchased a microcomputer together with stock and sales ledger programs. These packages are now in use but, for the time being, the other accounting systems remain entirely manual.

Your firm has recently been appointed as auditor of Kola Ltd and the directors have invited you to visit the company's premises and acquaint yourself with the company's activities and accounting systems.   They have also asked for your advice on appropriate control procedures for the microcomputer based accounting systems.

You ascertain that the microcomputer comprises a monitor, a Pentium system unit, a printer and a 20 Gb hard disk. The sales ledger and stock packages were purchased from a small software house on the advice of Tom's friend. The latter is a sole trader who is in a similar, but smaller, line of business to Kola Ltd.

The microcomputer is the responsibility of Anne Hughes, the cashier and bookkeeper who has worked for Kola Ltd for one year. Anne is assisted in the office by two accounts clerks.

The microcomputer is kept on Anne's desk. She tells you that the hard disk is backed up to DAT tape every Friday. The tape is kept in her office drawer next to the locked petty cash box.

As you discuss the system with Anne, Fred Sims enters her office and opens an account for a new customer. You note that the password, an 8 digit number, is sellotaped to the monitor. No printout of this transaction is obtained. He has also just received a large cheque from a customer and he posts it on to the sales ledger as he wishes to bank it immediately. He leaves a note of the customer and cheque amount on Anne's desk so that she can enter it into the manual cash book later in the day.

Anne confirms that anyone in the office can use the microcomputer as it is there to reduce her workload. She admits that the control accounts do not always balance, but she presumes that this is something 'the auditors can sort out at the year end'.

The warehouse supervisor updates the computerised stock records daily after Anne has finished work for the day. Tom Simms informs you that the supervisor carries out monthly test counts, agreeing physical stock to stock records. He has not been informed by the supervisor that there are any problems. He tells you that he doesn't see why you can't reduce your audit work as you can rely on the accuracy of the computer.

Task 1

Write a letter to Tom Simms explaining why audit planning is especially important where microcomputer based accounting systems are involved; highlight your explanations by using examples from Kola Ltd.

Task 2

Following your letter Tom agrees with your explanations and asks you to advise him of suitable control procedures that they could establish within the accounting system to ensure accuracy of the data.

---

2   Activity

Appendex Ltd merchandises ladies footwear. The company purchases the bulk of its goods from British suppliers and uses a system of networked PCs to record its business transactions. The computer department is located in the same office as the purchasing department and comprises the following personnel:

(i)   Mr Southfork, a systems analyst and programmer who is in charge of the department.

(ii)   Mrs Greenwood, a skilled programmer who also acts as a machine operator when the department is busy.

(iii)   Miss Wood, an assistant programmer and operator.

The computer software was purchased from a software house and was modified solely by Mr Southfork who kept the results of the testing of the modified programs for security reasons.

The purchasing department is managed by Mr Barnes, who is solely responsible for the placing of footwear orders. Purchase orders are provisionally fixed by telephone with suppliers and confirmed by Mr Barnes by fax. Mr Barnes lists the orders placed on a weekly basis and this list is used to update the stock file. The lead time between ordering and receipt of goods is normally fourteen days.

On receipt of the goods, the warehouseman makes out a prenumbered four-part goods received note set. One copy is given to the carrier as evidence of delivery of the goods, one copy each is sent to the purchasing department and the accounts department, whilst the final copy remains in the warehouse. Goods received notes are sent directly to Mr Barnes in the purchasing department.

When the accounts department receives the invoice, it is sent to Mr Barnes to authorise it and he checks the details to a copy of the fax order, and the goods received note. Further, after he has checked the details, he gives the documents to a member of his staff who checks the arithmetical accuracy of the invoice. If there is any discrepancy between it and the order and the goods received note, Mr Barnes alters the invoice by hand, and sends the invoice back to the accounts department who enter the amended amount on the purchase ledger input document which is sent to Mr Southfork.

On a weekly basis, Mrs Greenwood or Miss Wood updates the purchase ledger file which is held on the network server's hard disk and updates it from the input documentation received from the accounts department. The purchase ledger and an age listing of creditors is printed out once a month, and the stock ledger twice a month. These printouts are sent in the first instance to Mr Barnes who reviews them. Any exceptions which are apparent either in the review of the purchase ledger and stock file or because of processing problems are re-input only after Mr Barnes has given his authority. If input is rejected because there is no purchase ledger account on the disk, then Mr Southfork sets up an account and re-inputs the data himself.

Mr Southfork feels that he is very security conscious and dumps the files on the server's hard disk on to DAT tape on a weekly basis. This tape is kept in his desk drawer, and after one week the tape is overwritten. Mr Barnes determines which creditors are to be paid by making a manual listing of payments which is sent to the cashier. The cashier compares this listing to a copy of the purchase ledger print-out in order to verify the authenticity of the amount, and manually makes out the cheques which are signed by two directors. The directors scrutinise the listing of creditors for payment, before signing the cheques, and refuse to authorise any payment unless this listing has been signed by Mr Barnes and the cashier. Once the cheques have been signed, the payments listing is coded on to input documentation and sent to the computer department for processing. Any rejections of payment data are referred back to Mr Barnes who reviews the reason for the rejection, corrects it and re-inputs the data.

If goods are returned to the suppliers, a goods returns note is made out by the warehouseman in duplicate. One copy is returned with the goods, and the other copy is retained in the warehouse. When a credit note is received directly by Mr Barnes, he authorises it and the accounts department includes the value on the purchase invoice input sheet, and indicates the fact that it is a credit note by entering the amount in red ink on the list.

Task 1

Prepare a weakness schedule detailing the control weaknesses in the computer department together with the effects/implications of those weaknesses and suitable recommendations for their improvement.

(The weakness schedule should be split into two sections, one headed 'General Controls' and the other 'Application Controls'.)

Task 2

Prepare a weakness schedule detailing the weaknesses in the purchases and creditors system and make recommendations for their improvement (assume that the only controls are those stated above).

---

3   Activity

Your work in the audit of Appendex Ltd has identified the following problems:

- There are a number of supplier statements which do not agree with the balances on the purchase ledger print out. You have attempted to reconcile the statements to the purchase ledger balances without any success. The total number of statements which could not be reconciled was 15 out of a sample of 50 statements in the test.

- The monthly printouts of the purchase ledger had not been kept by the company but had been destroyed. This procedure had been instigated since the last audit by Mr Barnes who told you that only the current purchase ledger print-out was required by him, and that any other print-outs were superfluous to his requirements.

Task

Prepare a working paper for inclusion in the current file which explains the audit significance of the above instances.

Chapters 16-18

THE FINAL AUDIT

---

1   Activity

Lake Foundry is a small company producing aluminium and copper components for local industrialists. The company uses traditional methods of manufacture and is managed by Mr W Shore and his son Mr A Shore. The ordinary share capital is owned equally by the two men and the company is at present going through a transitional stage, whereby Mr W Shore is retiring from the business and transferring the majority of his shareholding to his son. The company employs 24 persons and has an annual turnover of £650,000.

The accounting records comprise a memorandum cash book, nominal ledger, sales and purchase ledgers. At present, sales orders, which are normally received on the telephone, are recorded in a two-part delivery note book only when the order has been produced and is ready for despatch to the customer. When the goods are delivered, one part of the delivery note is given to the customer and the other part remains in the book.

The sales orders are normally for small quantities of goods and because of this, the sales invoice is produced from the delivery note book at the end of each month. Mr A Shore agrees a price for the job with each customer and writes this price on the delivery note. The invoice is produced and posted to the sales ledger by Mrs V Shore, Mr A Shore's wife, at the end of each month. Mrs Shore is responsible for the maintenance of all accounting records other than wages, which are produced and prepared by a wages clerk.

The company costs its products in the following way:

For example:

	Job No 123 £
Cost of raw material	
5kg at £10 per kg	50.00
Labour, overhead and profit	
25% of raw material cost	12.50
	———
Selling price	62.50
	———

Mr A Shore normally purchases raw materials by telephoning the order to their suppliers. When the goods are received, Mr A Shore checks that the goods are correct as regards their quantity and type, and passes the supplier's goods received note to Mrs V Shore. When the supplier's invoice is received, it is posted immediately to the purchase ledger by Mrs V Shore. The company normally pays its creditors at the end of the month following the receipt of the purchase invoice, which is scrutinised by Mr A Shore when signing cheques.

The company does not produce monthly management or financial information. The management is worried about the lack of growth of the company and wishes to expand the business.

You have recently been appointed as auditor of the company for the year ended 31 March 20X8 and having ascertained and tested the system of internal control, you are about to prepare the management letter.

Task

Prepare a management letter for Lake Foundry Ltd, incorporating in your letter weaknesses and recommendations for improvements in the internal control system of the company.

Ensure the letter refers to the following items:

* Its purpose

* The level of management controls including recommendations for additional informational and organisational controls, and also the implications of the impending retirement of Mr W Shore

* Sales and debtors

* Purchases and creditors

---

2   Activity

A Statement of Auditing Standards has been issued on 'Management Representations'. You are the manager in charge of the audit of Lambley Properties plc and you have been asked to prepare the letter of representation which will be signed by the company's directors.

You are aware that there are two material items in the accounts for the year ended 31 January 20X3 on which you want the company's directors to confirm that the treatment in the accounts is correct:

(a)   One of the company's subsidiaries, Keyworth Builders Ltd, is experiencing going concern problems, and you want the directors' confirmation that they intend to support the company for the foreseeable future.

(b)   Eastwood Manufacturing plc is in dispute with Lambley Properties over repairs required to a building they purchased from Lambley. Lambley Properties constructed the building for Eastwood, and three years after it was sold to Eastwood, the customer is claiming that repairs are required which will cost £3 million, and that Lambley is liable to pay for these repairs, as they are as a result of negligent construction of the building. In addition, Eastwood is claiming £2 million for the cost of disruption of its business due to the faults in the building and in the period when the repairs take place. Lambley Properties has not included any provision in its accounts for this claim. Lambley Properties have obtained the advice of a lawyer and a surveyor, and the directors believe there are no grounds for the claim and any court action will find in their favour. However, Lambley Properties has included a note in its accounts concerning this contingency.

Task 1

Prepare a letter of representation for the directors to sign and send to you as auditors. In the letter you should include the two items above in addition to any other matters which you consider should be included.

Task 2

Explain to the junior auditor assisting you with the work the reliability of a letter of representation as audit evidence and the extent to which an auditor can rely on this evidence.

Task 3

Prepare an audit programme detailing the procedures you would perform to check whether a provision should be included in the accounts for the legal claim from Eastwood Manufacturing plc.

3   Activity

You are engaged in the final examination of the financial statements of Birchinlee plc for the year to 30 June 20X4, a company engaged in the purchase and resale of earthenware and crockery products. You are aware that the company has increased its trading activity substantially during the year, that it has plans for future expansion and that it intends to request a considerable extension in overdraft facilities with its bank following issue of the audited financial statements.

Summarised draft financial statements for the year to 30 June 20X4, together with comparative figures are set out below.

Profit and loss account

	20X4		20X3	
	£	£	£	£
Turnover		24,000,000		13,875,000
Cost of sales		(14,500,000)		(9,712,500)
Gross profit		9,500,000		4,162,500
Distribution costs	(3,280,000)		(1,110,000)	
Administrative expenses	(1,300,000)		(1,200,000)	
Loss on disposal of fixed assets	(2,000,000)		(200,000)	
Interest payable	(80,000)		-	
Income from trade investments	50,000		75,000	
		(6,610,000)		(2,435,000)
Profit before taxation		2,890,000		1,727,500
Taxation		(300,000)		(900,000)
Profit after taxation		2,590,000		827,500
Dividends proposed		(150,000)		(150,000)
Profit retained		2,440,000		677,500
Profit brought forward		5,720,000		5,042,500
		8,160,000		5,720,000

	£	£
Depreciation has been included in the above headings as follows:		
Cost of sales	180,000	140,000
Distribution costs	60,000	50,000
Administrative expenses	60,000	50,000
	300,000	240,000

Balance sheet

	20X4			20X3		
	Cost £	Dep'n £	Balance £	Cost £	Dep'n £	Balance £
Fixed assets:						
Tangible assets*	4,300,000	530,000	3,770,000	5,000,000	1,330,000	3,670,000
Trade investments			2,600,000			2,600,000
			6,370,000			6,270,000
Current assets:						
Stock	4,500,000			1,500,000		
Trade debtors	3,900,000			1,700,000		
Bank	-			400,000		
	8,400,000			3,600,000		
Current liabilities:						
Trade creditors	(3,500,000)			(1,100,000)		
Taxation	(300,000)			(900,000)		
Dividends	(150,000)			(150,000)		
Bank overdraft	(660,000)			-		
		(4,610,000)			(2,150,000)	
Net current assets			3,790,000			1,450,000
Net assets employed			10,160,000			7,720,000
Financed by:						
Share capital			2,000,000			2,000,000
Profit and loss account			8,160,000			5,720,000
			10,160,000			7,720,000

* A tangible asset generally is one that can be touched - land, buildings, plant and equipment, etc.

Cash Flow Statement

	£	£
Net cash inflow from operating activities (note 1)		2,420,000
Returns on investments and servicing of finance		
Interest received	50,000	
Interest paid	(80,000)	
Net cash outflow from returns on investments and servicing of finance		(30,000)
		2,390,000
Taxation		
Corporation tax paid	(900,000)	
Tax paid		(900,000)
		1,490,000
Capital expenditure		
Payments to acquire tangible fixed assets	(2,500,000)	
Receipts from sales of tangible fixed assets	100,000	
Net cash outflow from capital expenditure		(2,400,000)
		(910,000)
Equity dividends paid		(150,000)
Decrease in cash		(1,060,000)

Notes to the cash flow statement

(1)   Reconciliation of operating profit to net cash inflow from operating activities

	£	£
Operating profit	2,890,000	
Adjustment for investing activities:		
Interest received	(50,000)	
Interest paid	80,000	
		2,920,000
Depreciation charges		300,000
Loss on sale of tangible fixed assets		2,000,000
Increase in stocks		(3,000,000)
Increase in debtors		(2,200,000)
Increase in creditors		2,400,000
Net cash inflow from operating activities		2,420,000

(2)   Analysis of changes in cash during the year

	£
Opening balance	400,000
Net cash outflow	(1,060,000)
Closing balance	(660,000)

(3)   Analysis of balances of cash as shown in the balance sheet

			Change in
	20X4	20X3	year
	£	£	£
Cash at bank and in hand	-	400,000	(400,000)
Bank overdrafts	(660,000)	-	(660,000)
			(1,060,000)

Task 1

Review the draft financial statements and note four matters that you will raise (and reasons why) with the directors at your forthcoming meeting.

Task 2

Prepare a questionnaire with issues to raise with the directors specifying two questions for each of the four matters raised in Task 1.

Task 3

Prior to your meeting one of the directors leaves a message with your secretary asking you to call him and explain exactly why it is necessary for you to perform an analytical review and what purpose it achieves.

Document a suitable response prior to returning his call.

---

4   Activity

You are one of the audit partners in a firm of accountants and are currently dealing with the audits of three of your clients. You have just returned from a meeting with the other partners and your secretary has given you messages from each of the clients with details of actions they propose to take; these actions have a bearing on the audit and are as follows:

(a)   Taggart Ltd are brandy distillers and normally hold stock for six years before selling it. A large quantity of two-year-old stock has been sold to Cloves plc, a merchant bank, at cost plus 5% profit. The company's normal selling price is cost plus 50%. Taggart Ltd has an option to buy back the brandy in four years time at a price which represents the original sale price plus interest at the current market rate. The stock has remained on the premises of Taggart Ltd, but has been recorded as a sale in their financial statements.

(b)   The directors of Wolfworld Ltd have decided to incorporate a revaluation of the whole of its fixed assets into its financial records. The existing policy of depreciating assets on a reducing balance basis is to be continued but the total depreciation charge for each category of assets will be divided between the amount based on historical cost and the additional amount arising as a result of the revaluation. The latter amount is to be charged against the revaluation reserve leaving only the historical cost charge in the profit and loss account.

(c)   The directors of Basnet plc have decided not to publish a cash flow statement in the financial statements on the grounds that users may be confused by the statement.

Task

Write letters to the directors of each of the three companies i.e. Taggart Ltd, Wolfworld Ltd and Basnet plc explaining the audit implications of each of the situations.

Indicate in the letters the reasons why there is an audit problem and suggest solutions which would ensure the truth and fairness of the financial statements.

Chapters 19-20

AUDITOR'S LIABILITY AND CURRENT ISSUES

---

1   Activity

You are the manager of the audit team which has recently completed the audit of X Ltd, a shoe manufacturing and importing company, which has one central factory and warehouse and 32 retail branches spread throughout the country and which only receive stock from the central warehouse. All accounting records are maintained at the head office which is on the same site as the factory and warehouse. Control of the branches is achieved by recording all stock movements and sales at selling price.

An example of a week's transactions would be as follows:

	All at selling price £
Opening stock at branch	25,000
Transfers to branch from warehouse	14,500
Sales for week (cash banked)	(15,000)
Closing stock counted by branch staff or internal audit staff	24,500

Since opening stock, transfers from warehouse and sales (cash banked) are all known, the theoretical closing stock can easily be calculated and compared with that actually counted to establish gains or losses. The company has an internal audit department and part of their work is to observe stocktakes at branches on a rotational basis. You have reviewed the work of the internal audit department and have satisfied yourself that it is an effective tool of management and that it forms a reliable part of the whole system of internal control. The company's total year-end stock in the central warehouse and branches is valued at £2.6 million and each branch holds between £20,000 and £30,000 of stock. The audit team has tested the existence and satisfactory operation of internal controls by visiting ten branches. The audit team attended the factory/warehouse stocktake and the stocktake at a further ten branches (the ten being chosen out of the 32 on a rotational basis). You had concluded that the stocktaking was carried out satisfactorily and you (at the close of the audit field work) were of the opinion that the company's stock was fairly valued. Prior to the partner in charge of the audit signing the audit opinion the finance director of the company telephoned to say that the internal audit department had found that the physical stock at one branch was less than the book quantities and the manager had admitted misappropriating company footwear and falsifying the stock records.

You had carried out tests on the internal controls at the branch which was subject to audit during the year.

The finance director is of the opinion that, while the theft is not material in the context of this year's financial statements, your firm has been negligent in its audit approach.

Task 1

Write a letter to the Finance Director explaining who the auditor has a duty to in relation to a statutory audit, and what his duties are. Ensure your letter incorporates reference to relevant case law and give at least two examples of best audit practice.

Task 2

Following receipt of your letter the Finance Director wishes to meet with you to discuss the issues; he has also asked you to prepare a report outlining the auditor's duty to detect fraud, and relate your report to the situation that has occurred within X Ltd.

Draft this report. This should be in the form of an executive summary, rather than a full report format.

---

2   Activity

A Statement of Auditing Standards has been issued on 'Considering the work of internal audit'. You have recently been appointed auditor of Hyson Hotels plc which owns and runs about 100 hotels in the UK. The company has an established internal audit department, which both operates at the head office and visits the hotels.

Each hotel has a computer which records the bookings of rooms for overnight accommodation and the accounts for each guest.

Prior to commencement of the audit you have scheduled a meeting with the Head of Internal Audit.

Task 1

Write a letter to the Head of Internal Audit informing him of the work you would have expected the Internal Audit Department to have been carrying out to date. Include details in your letter of the effect it would have on your audit work should you decide that you can rely on the work of Internal Audit.

Task 2

Prepare an audit programme detailing the work you would perform to enable you to assess the extent to which you could rely on the work of the internal auditors.

(Add any additional supplementary factors you would consider as part of this assessment on a separate working paper.)

---

3   Activity

You have just commenced employment with the Association of Accounting Technicians; they have asked you to write an article for the students newsletter as it has become apparent that students seem to be finding the area of auditor's liability confusing. In addition the accountancy profession itself is constantly concerned by the problem of auditor's liability.

Task

Write an article for the newsletter which considers the following issues:

- the parties to whom the auditor might be liable
- the circumstances under which the auditor might be liable to third parties
- possible defences for the auditor in the event that a liability claim arises.

PRACTICE DEVOLVED ASSESSMENTS

QUESTIONS

◈ **FOULKS**lynch

FOULKS*lynch*

TECHNICIAN STAGE

NVQ/SVQ LEVEL 4 IN ACCOUNTING

PRACTICE DEVOLVED ASSESSMENT 1

IMPLEMENTING AUDITING PROCEDURES

(UNIT 17)

THE SITUATION:

You are one of three audit seniors employed by Heaton, Brooking & Co. a small firm of accountants. You are currently assisting in the audit of a small/medium sized private limited company *'Spicer Cuts'* which owns a chain of four hairdressing salons in a large city, one of which is the Head Office and the other three are smaller branches.

You have one junior auditor Jane Brown working for you on this audit. The year end you are auditing is year ended 30 September 20X8.

The Audit Manager to whom you report has had a meeting with the client, and now has a number of tasks which she would like you to complete.

These tasks are detailed on pages 105 and 106.

The Company's profit for the last year is detailed in *Appendix A*, together with the Balance Sheet. The Company's profit has risen steadily over the last five years by approximately 5% per annum.

TASKS TO BE COMPLETED:

1   Read the permanent information on pages 117 to 119 of the answer booklet in order to obtain a clear understanding of the client's background and situation.

Using the Manager's meeting notes (refer Appendix B) from her discussions with the client:

(i)   Update the permanent information on pages 117 to 119 of the answer booklet

(ii)   On a separate working paper (using pages 120 and 121 of the answer booklet) explain what inherent risk is and detail what you consider to be the inherent risks in Spicer Cuts Ltd.

2   Jane Brown has told you she doesn't understand the reasons for updating the permanent file, and said that she doesn't see the point in maintaining any files other than the current file. She commented that it just seems to be creating extra work.

• Using the blank memorandum on page 122 of your answer booklet, write a reply to Jane explaining the difference between the permanent and current files, and give examples of the types of information retained in each of them.

3   Using the Internal Control Evaluation Questionnaire (ICEQ) form on pages 123 to 126 of the answer booklet detail the Control Questions required to be answered to establish whether specific errors/frauds are possible in the sales system and the stock system (NB : the two systems should be considered in isolation and the answers provided on different pages).

4   Using the audit programmes on pages 127 and 128 of the answer booklet, and the information contained in Appendix E – Extract 'Fixed Asset Ledger' detail the substantive tests which should be undertaken to confirm the following:

(i)   Completeness, existence, valuation and ownership of fixed assets

(ii)   The accuracy of the depreciation amount

5   Using the working papers on pages 129 and 130 of the answer booklet detail the audit procedures that would be conducted to ascertain whether or not the client's stocktaking instructions are adequate.

6   Using the audit programmes on pages 131 to 133 of the answer booklet describe the tests you would perform to ensure that controls are sufficient to prevent material fraud/error in the cash sales system

7   (i)   Using the creditors ledger information in Appendix C and the creditors statements in Appendix D, reconcile the two using the working paper on page 134 in the answer booklet. Any differences found should be clearly documented. (NOTE: You can assume that the information on the creditors statements has been verified as correct)

(ii)   Complete the weakness schedule on page 135 of the answer booklet explaining the significance of the results of your test in 7(i).

(iii)   Using the working paper on page 136 of the answer booklet state what further action you might take as a result of the weaknesses you have found and also as part of your normal creditors testing.

8   Using the weakness schedules on pages 137 to 138 of the answer booklet describe the weaknesses n controls within Spicer Cuts computer system, and make recommendations for improvements explaining the reasons for such improvements. You should assume that the only controls are those described.

◈ FOULKS*lynch*

9   Jane is currently working on tests in respect of Spicer Cuts Payroll system; you visit her at the clients to discuss a number of issues. When you arrive you find that Jane has not yet arrived, however, all her payroll working papers are on the desk that she is using at the clients (which is situated in the staff room) together with a copy of the payroll report she is currently working on. Her laptop, containing all the audit working papers on it is also on the desk, and hasn't been switched off since the day before. You also note that her password is written on a post-it attached to the laptop. She finally arrives 1 hour late apologising for the delay due to the traffic being busy at that time in the morning.

Detail on the audit working papers on pages 139 and 140 of the answer booklet the following:

- The points you would raise with Jane, and why, in respect of the above incident
- The action(s) you might take for the remainder of the audit, and
- The overall recommendation you would make to the Audit Manager regarding this matter.

10   Using the weakness schedule completed for question 8 (re: computer system weaknesses), set out three points to be included in the management letter together with the relevant implications for each weakness, and recommendations for improvement. Use page 141 of the answer booklet.

APPENDIX A

Spicer Cuts Ltd
Balance Sheet as at 30 September 20X8

Fixed Assets	£000	£000
Fixtures and Fittings		60
Salon Equipment		7
Computer Equipment		5
		72
Current Assets		
Stock	5	
Prepayments	2	
Bank	75	
Cash	1	
	83	
Creditors less than 1 year:		
Trade Creditors	12	
Other Creditors	10	
Bank Loan	8	
	30	
Net Current Assets		53
Net Assets		125
Share Capital	75	
Profit and Loss Account	50	
		125

Spicer Cuts Ltd
Summary Profit and Loss Account for year ended 30 September 20X8

	£
Sales	500,000
Cost of Sales	100,000
Gross Profit	**400,000**
Expenses	200,000
Net Profit	**200,000**

APPENDIX B

Client:	Spicer Cuts Ltd	**W/P REF**:	A1/1
Accounting Date:	30/9/X8		

Prepared By:	RRT
Date:	2/1/X9
Reviewed By:	GL
Date:	2/1/X9

Meeting Notes:

Present: RRT   Audit Manager
Neil Spicer, Managing Director, Spicer Cuts Ltd
Christine Spicer, Personnel Director, Spicer Cuts Ltd
Ms Sandra Grant, Accountant, Spicer Cuts Ltd

Turnover has increased since the previous year, again showing a steady growth on previous years of 5%. Due to this 2 more junior stylists have been appointed at Head Office, one reporting to each of the Senior Stylists, and one more at each of the other salons.

Neil stated that there had been a few problems at one of the Salon's as the Stylist in Charge had left and the new one had considered a lot of the procedures unnecessary and hadn't maintained the records up to date. This had now been rectified, and things were starting to improve however, there were still a few morale problems.

Neil also stated that the introduction of the computer system seemed to be causing a few stock problems as for the last six months the actual stock had not agreed with the stock records, and the deficit was increasing each month.

Neil also mentioned that one of the salon's PCs had been stolen recently which they had now replaced but they had lost all their client information as back ups hadn't been performed. He mentioned that automatic backups were now taken every day via the server and stored off site at a local computer company – this storage facility had been set up for all salons.

Sandra stated that there had been a problem with general cash sales (not stock) whereby a couple of times she had had more money than sales that had been recorded on the computer system, and also sometimes more sales had been recorded than she had cash for. She said she was very concerned at the very informal approach staff seemed to take towards such important procedures, seeing them very much as an unnecessary chore. Sandra also added that she now produced a cash flow forecast for the financial year as part of her management reports, and her and Neil now had a weekly ½ hour meeting on the last Friday of each month to discuss these.

Christine stated that all staff salaries are now paid direct into their bank accounts; this is actioned by her from home. The procedure is that she faxes the bank with the relevant details on a standard form supplied by the Bank five days before payment is due; they then return an acknowledgement which is checked by her and any adjustments must be made within 48 hours.

Neil stated that the computers at all the salons had now been networked to the Head Office computers; Christine's PC has also been connected to the network – the networking was completed two months ago and they were looking into trying to improve the security as they thought there were improvements that could be made on the current system which had not changed since the PCs were first installed. The management information from each salon was now emailed to Head Office

Neil also commented that the petty cash balance had now been increased to £200 as a couple of the Stylists in Charge had complained that £100 wasn't enough. Petty cash records have now been computerised and expenditure details are then emailed to Head Office.

Neil also added that one of the salons has been experiencing problems with some of their regular customers whereby a number of cheques have been returned unpaid and the customer has not re-visited the salon.

APPENDIX C

SUMMARY AGED CREDITORS LISTING AS AT 30 SEPTEMBER 20X8:

CREDITOR NAME	TOTAL BALANCE	CURRENT	>30 DAYS	>60 DAYS	>90 DAYS
	£	£	£	£	£
Split Enz Ltd	1456.53	1456.53			
Huriel Hair Products	nil				
Conditioners & Co Ltd	950.24	700.24	250.00		
Jazzy Dryers plc	109.50	109.50			
Solely Computers	175.00		175.00		
Sunnie Holidays	4012.59	4012.59			
Pete's Plumbers	850.43	850.43			
Cheapy Wholesalers	601.45	601.45			
Hair for Your Needs	953.46	50.00	903.46		
Luxury Towels Ltd	1500.78	1500.78			
	10609.98	9281.52	1328.46		

Note: **All** *Spicer Cuts creditors included within their accounts are shown above*

APPENDIX D

SUPPLIER STATEMENTS:

You find the following supplier statements relating to Spicer Cuts creditors in Ms Grant's 'post in' file:

SPLIT ENZ LTD

STATEMENT

Spicer Cuts Ltd

Date: 30/09/X8

	£
B/F from previous statement	483.96
Invoice SC/98/1485	54.29
Invoice SC/98/1587	251.92
Invoice SC/98/1652	1150.32
Payment received	(483.96)
Invoice SC/98/1741	360.25
TOTAL DUE	**1816.78**

HURIEL HAIR PRODUCTS

STATEMENT

Spicer Cuts Ltd

Date: 30/09/X8

B/F from previous statement	£1,600.89

**PAYMENT OVERDUE; IF NOT RECEIVED IN 7 DAYS LEGAL ACTION
WILL BE TAKEN**

CONDITIONERS & CO LTD

STATEMENT

Spicer Cuts Ltd

Date: 30/09/X8

	£	£
B/F from previous statement		**500.46**
Invoice 19562	165.22	
Payment Received	(250.00)	
Invoice 20456	84.78	
Invoice 21222	700.24	
Payment received	(250.46)	
Invoice 22678	130.91	
(500.46)	**1581.61**	
TOTAL NOW DUE		*1081.15*

JAZZY DRYERS PLC

STATEMENT

SPICER CUTS LTD

DATE: 30TH SEPTEMBER 20X8

	£	£
B/F FROM PREVIOUS STATEMENT		109.50
	£	
INVOICE 216	54.75	
INVOICE 245	54.75	
INVOICE 291	54.75	
INVOICE 312	54.75	
		219.00
PAYMENT RECEIVED		(164.25)
BALANCE DUE		164.25

STATEMENT

SOLELY Computers

Spicer Cuts Ltd

Date: 30/09/X8

	£
B/F from previous statement	NIL
Invoice 098156/2	175.00
Invoice 098256/1	58.23
TOTAL DUE	**234.23**

SUNNIE HOLIDAYS

STATEMENT

Spicer Cuts Ltd

Date: 30th September 20X8

	£
Invoice 9809/456	4012.59

PAYMENT NOW DUE

Pete's Plumbers

STATEMENT

Spicer Cuts Ltd

Date: 30/09/X8

	£
B/F from previous statement	NIL
Invoice 015671	850.43
Invoice 015678	60.22
TOTAL	**910.65**

Cheapy Wholesalers

STATEMENT

Spicer Cuts Ltd

Date: 30/09/X8

	£	£
B/F from previous statement		398.93
Invoice		153.61
Invoice		22.75
Invoice		54.88
Payment received	403.83	
Invoice		375.11
TOTAL		**601.45**

HAIR FOR YOUR NEEDS

STATEMENT

Spicer Cuts Ltd

Date: 30th September 20X8

	£	£
B/F from previous statement		1803.46
Invoice 01523		50.23
Payment Received	99.58	
Payment Received	800.42	
TOTAL		**953.69**

LUXURY TOWELS LTD

STATEMENT

Spicer Cuts Ltd

Date: 30/09/X8

	£
B/F from previous statement	1200.21
Invoice SC/00240	200.00
Invoice SC/00256	100.57
Invoice SC/00278	53.21
TOTAL NOW DUE	1553.99

On making enquiries of Sandra Grant, the Accountant, in respect of your work on Creditors you obtain the following information:

1   The invoice for Sunnie Holidays cannot be found; Ms Grant stated that she could not remember what it was for, she just pays all invoices passed to her.

2   The amount of £1600.89 due to Huriel Hair Products has not been paid as Spicer Cuts were not happy with the quality of the goods and returned them – Huriel Hair products have stated that they never received them and are now threatening court action. Ms Grant tells you that she's not sure what to do and is waiting to discuss it with Mr Neil Spicer; although at the moment he's very busy and never seems to have a spare minute.

3   Ms Grant tells you that she never usually looks at the creditors statements as she relies on the accuracy of the accounts and doesn't have time to check the statements as well as everything else she has to do.

APPENDIX E

SPICER CUTS LTD

FIXED ASSET REGISTER – EXTRACT

ASSET NO.	PURCHASE DATE	PURCHASE PRICE £	DESCRIPTION	DEPN METHOD & RATE (notes)	DEPN IN YR £	TOTAL DEPN TO DATE £	NET BOOK VALUE £	LOCATION
00005	01/11/V1	800.00	Sink units for H Office	RB 15%	Nil	800.00	Nil	H Office
00006	06/12/V1	500.00	Hairdryers x 2	SL 10%	Nil	500.00	Nil	H Office
00012	03/11/V2	600.00	Built in wardrobe	RB 15%	Nil	600.00	Nil	H Office
00025	05/06/V6	450.00	Desk unit	RB 15%	Nil	450.00	Nil	H Office
00029	18/11/V9	300.00	Hairdryer x 1	SL 10%	30.00	570.00	Nil	H Office
00039	22/07/W1	1200.00	Sink units for Salon 2	RB 15%	Nil	1200.00	Nil	Salon 2
00050	15/03/W8	150.00	Filing cabinet	SL 10%	15.00	165.00	(15.00)	Salon 3
00061	19/09/X1	400.00	Hairdryer x 1	SL 10%	40.00	320.00	80.00	Salon 3
00099	12/07/X7	2250.00	Sink units for Salon 4	RB 15%	287.00	624.50	1625.50	Salon 4
00109	31/03/X8	1500.00	Computer equipment	SL 25%	375.00	375.00	1125.00	H Office
00116	15/04/X8	1200.00	Computer equipment	SL 25%	300.00	300.00	900.00	H Office
00124	01/05/X8	850.00	Computer equipment	SL 25%	212.50	212.50	637.50	Salon 1

Notes: RB = Reducing Balance
SL = Straight Line
The total number of assets held at year end totalled 124
Assets 6 and 29 were sold in the year to a local technical college

IMPLEMENTING AUDITING PROCEDURES

ANSWER BOOKLET

TASK 1(i)

EXTRACT FROM PERMANENT FILE

BACKGROUND INFORMATION

Spicer Cuts Ltd was formed in 20V1 by Mr Neil Spicer and his wife Christine both of whom were the principal stylists. The company has expanded rapidly since then with the establishment of three further branches. Christine no longer acts as a stylist but works principally from home undertaking all personnel related tasks.

The organisation structure of the firm's head office (and principal salon) is as follows:

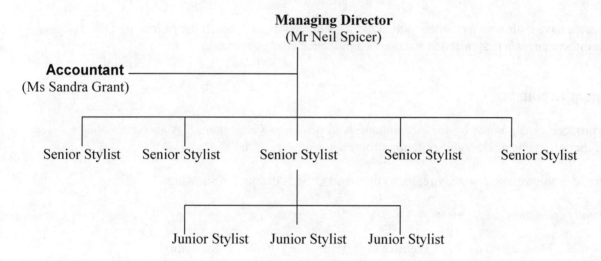

The Company Shareholders and Directors are:

Mr Neil Spicer	Managing Director	(50%)	
Mrs Christine Spicer	Personnel Director	(50%)	*Wife of Managing Director*

Mrs Spicer works primarily from home, where the personnel records are kept, and also runs the payroll each month.

None of the three other salons has a Managing Director and comprises 1 Stylist in Charge, 3 Senior Stylists and 1 Junior Stylist. The Stylist in Charge reports to the Managing Director, and all four have a meeting once a week to discuss relevant issues. In addition, Mr Neil Spicer visits each of the salons once a week on a Monday morning.

The Company's profit for the last year is detailed in *Appendix A*, together with the Balance Sheet. The Company's profit has risen steadily over the last five years by approximately 5% per annum.

ACCOUNTING SYSTEM

Computer Environment

The salons did not have any computer facilities until August 20X7 when the Managing Director decided to invest a substantial amount of money to save time and improve management information. Prior to this, all functions were totally manual.

The Head Office has two PCs:

PC 1 which can be accessed by the Accountant (and is located in her office) and Managing Director and contains accounting information only.

PC 2 is used for recording stock movements, customer information (a record is held for each customer) and appointments and can be accessed by the Managing Director and any of the Stylists.

The other three salons have one PC which can be accessed by the Stylist in Charge and the Senior Stylists; and are used to record stock movements and information necessary to complete the weekly returns (see next section 'Management Accounts') for Head Office. A standard software package is used for the accounting records. A separate system designed for salons (also a standard software package) is used to record stock movements etc.

There is no maintenance contract in place.

It is up to the Senior Stylist and Managing Director to remember to take backups. The backup disks are retained in the drawer on the reception desk. The Accountant does not currently take backups.

All of the users have their own password (which is their christian name) which the Managing Director gave them when the system was first installed – these have not been changed since.

Management Accounts

These are produced each month by the Accountant, who produces a profit and loss account, balance sheet for each of the salons and also combined reports for the business as a whole.

Each of the three salons send a weekly return to the Head Office Accountant showing:

1   *Details of Takings, as follows:*

	Monday	**Tuesday**	**Wednesday**	**Thursday**	**Friday**	**Saturday**
Cash Takings:						
Cheque Takings:						

2   *Details of Stock Used / Sold, as follows:*

Stock Used:	**Stock Sold to Customers** (at 25% Mark Up)	**Stock Sold to Staff**
Shampoo		
Conditioner		
Styling Mousse		
Hairspray		
Permanent		
Colouring		

Sales and Debtors

Sales are either by cash or cheque – the MD is currently considering accepting credit card, and debit card payments but has not yet made a decision. Cheques are usually supported by cheque card details, apart from where it is a regular customer and stylists usually veto this procedure, considering that they can rely on their knowledge of the customer. In addition, if a regular customer forgets their cheque book stylists permit them to post it in. It is up to the stylist to make a note of this and the sale will not be recorded until the cheque is received. Any tips received are put into a container by the till and shared equally at the end of each day.

It is up to each individual stylist to record their own 'sales' on the computer system ie amount and payment method against the client name. A print out of each sale is obtained at the time of sale and these are checked to the total sales report at the end of week by the MD if he has time.

If debtors exist at any time they are therefore usually for very small amounts.

Stock

Stock comprises hair products which are used in the salon, sold (at 25% mark up) to customers or sold to staff.

All stock items (refer to section on Management Accounts detailing different stock items) are controlled by Head Office who places all orders, using the weekly information received from each salon.

Stock sales are recorded separately to normal 'sales' using a different software package.

It is up to the individual stylist to record the sale of any stock items at the time of sale against the relevant client. All stylists at each of the salons have the ability to update the stock records.

When stock is received at Head Office, the Goods Received Note (GRN) is used to update the stock system; this is done by the MD. The MD then delivers the stock to the other three salons at his weekly visit.

A stock check is performed once a year by the MD and the Stylists in Charge. Any discrepancies are investigated by the MD.

Staff can purchase stock items at cost price; these must be prior approved by the MD.

Purchases and Creditors

The MD, or branch Stylists in Charge review the stock levels each week and faxes orders (using a standard order form) for replacement stock to the relevant suppliers.

When deliveries are received, these are checked to the faxed order by the MD. The GRN is used to update the stock system and then passed to the Accountant who matches it to the invoice.

All cheques are manually written out by the Accountant and can be authorised by her (up to £500). The MD or his wife has to authorise cheques above this amount. The MD and his wife also have a business cheque book at home.

The Accountant reconciles the Purchase Ledger Control Account at the end of each month to the Purchase Ledger. Purchase Ledger Accounts are also reconciled to the supplier statements when received.

Payroll

Mrs Spicer controls the payroll which is run monthly (at the end of each month) using her PC at home. She usually visits the Head Office at the end of each month to meet with the Accountant and give her the payroll reports which are kept in a locked cabinet together with the payslips. Payment is made to employees by cheques written by Mrs Spicer and then posted to each of the Salons.

Any casual work is paid for in cash.

Petty Cash

A petty cash balance of £100 is held at Head Office and each of the salons. This is checked by the MD at his weekly visit who reimburses the salon with the appropriate amount. He takes each of the salon's petty cash records for the week to the Head Office Accountant for input into the accounting system.

TASK 1(ii)

Client: **W/P REF:**
Accounting Date:

Prepared By:
Date:
Reviewed By:
Date:

TASK 1(ii)

Client:

Accounting Date:

W/P REF:

Prepared By:
Date:
Reviewed By:
Date:

TASK 2

MEMORANDUM

TO:

FROM: *REF:*

DATE:

SUBJECT:

TASK 3

Client: W/P REF:
Accounting Date:

                                                 Prepared By: ◇ FOULKS*lynch*
                                                 Date:
                                                 Reviewed By:
                                                 Date:

INTERNAL CONTROL EVALUATION QUESTIONNAIRE

TEST:

Control Objectives: (Not required as part of answer)

Business Considerations: (Not required as part of answer)

CONTROL QUESTIONS:	COMMENTS	W/P REF

TASK 3

Client:	**W/P REF**:
Accounting Date:	
	Prepared By:
	Date:
	Reviewed By:
	Date:

INTERNAL CONTROL EVALUATION QUESTIONNAIRE

TEST:

Control Objectives: (Not required as part of answer)

Business Considerations: (Not required as part of answer)

CONTROL QUESTIONS:	*COMMENTS*	*W/P REF*

TASK 3

Client:	**W/P REF**:
Accounting Date:	
	Prepared By:
	Date:
	Reviewed By:
	Date:

INTERNAL CONTROL EVALUATION QUESTIONNAIRE

TEST:

Control Objectives: (Not required as part of answer)

Business Considerations: (Not required as part of answer)

CONTROL QUESTIONS:	COMMENTS	W/P REF

TASK 3

Client: W/P REF:
Accounting Date:

                                             Prepared By:
                                             Date:
                                             Reviewed By:
                                             Date:

INTERNAL CONTROL EVALUATION QUESTIONNAIRE

TEST:

Control Objectives: (Not required as part of answer)

Business Considerations: (Not required as part of answer)

CONTROL QUESTIONS:	COMMENTS	W/P REF

TASK 4 (i)

Client:	Spicer Cuts Ltd
Accounting Date:	30/09/X8

W/P REF:	F1/1
Prepared By:	RRT
Date:	
Reviewed By:	GL
Date:	

AUDIT PROGRAMME

AUDIT TEST	WP REF	WORK PERFORMED BY

TASK 4(ii)

Client:	Spicer Cuts Ltd	**W/P REF**:	F1/1
Accounting Date:	30/09/X8		
		Prepared By:	RRT
		Date:	
		Reviewed By:	GL
		Date:	

AUDIT PROGRAMME

AUDIT TEST	WP REF	WORK PERFORMED BY

TASK 5

Client:	Spicer Cuts Ltd	**W/P REF**:	F1/1
Accounting Date:	30/09/X8		
		Prepared By:	RRT
		Date:	
		Reviewed By:	GL
		Date:	

TASK 5

Client:	Spicer Cuts Ltd	**W/P REF**:	F1/1
Accounting Date:	30/09/X8		
		Prepared By:	RRT
		Date:	
		Reviewed By:	GL
		Date:	

Client:	Spicer Cuts Ltd	**W/P REF**:	F1/1
Accounting Date:	30/09/X8		

◈ FOULKS*lynch*

TASK 6

Client:	Spicer Cuts Ltd
Accounting Date:	30/09/X8

W/P REF:	F1/1
Prepared By:	RRT
Date:	
Reviewed By:	GL
Date:	

AUDIT PROGRAMME

AUDIT TEST	WP REF	WORK PERFORMED BY

TASK 6

Client:	Spicer Cuts Ltd	**W/P REF**:	F1/1
Accounting Date:	30/09/X8		
		Prepared By:	RRT
		Date:	
		Reviewed By:	GL
		Date:	

AUDIT PROGRAMME

AUDIT TEST	WP REF	WORK PERFORMED BY

Client:	Spicer Cuts Ltd	**W/P REF**:	F1/1
Accounting Date:	30/09/X8		

TASK 6

Client: Spicer Cuts Ltd   **W/P REF**:
Accounting Date: 30/09/X8

                                                Prepared By: RRT
                                                Date:
                                                Reviewed By: GL
                                                Date:

AUDIT PROGRAMME

AUDIT TEST	WP	WORK PERFORMED BY	WORK REVIEWED BY

TASK 7(i)

Client:	**W/P REF:**
Accounting Date:	
	Prepared By:
	Date:
	Reviewed By:
	Date:

TEST:

OBJECTIVE:

TESTING PERFORMED:

RESULTS:

CONCLUSION:

TASK 7 (ii)

Client: Spicer Cuts Ltd
Accounting Date: 30/09/X8

W/P REF:
PREPARED BY:
DATE:
REVIEWED BY:
DATE:

EVALUATION SCHEDULE

WEAKNESS	W/P REF	IMPLICATIONS	RECOMMENDATIONBS

TASK 7 (iii)

Client: **W/P REF:**   F1/3

Accounting Date:

                                                     Prepared By:
                                                     Date:
                                                     Reviewed By:
                                                     Date:

Further Actions to be Taken:

TASK 8
Client: Spicer Cuts Ltd
Accounting Date: 30/09/X8

W/P REF:
PREPARED BY:
REVIEWED BY:

EVALUATION SCHEDULE

WEAKNESS	W/P REF	EFFECT	RECOMMMENDATIONS

TASK 8

Client: Spicer Cuts Ltd
Accounting Date: 30/09/X8

EVALUATION SCHEDULE

W/P REF:
PREPARED BY:
REVIEWED BY:

WEAKNESS	W/P REF	EFFECT	RECOMMENDATIONS

TASK 9

Client: **W/P REF**:
Accounting Date:

Prepared By:
Date:
Reviewed By:
Date:

TASK 9

Client: W/P REF:
Accounting Date:

                                                 Prepared By:
                                                 Date:
                                                 Reviewed By:
                                                 Date:

TASK 10

Management Letter Extract:

Heaton Brooking & Co
2 Main Road
Manchester
MU4 6HJ

TECHNICIAN STAGE

NVQ/SVQ LEVEL 4 IN ACCOUNTING

PRACTICE DEVOLVED ASSESSMENT 2

IMPLEMENTING AUDITING PROCEDURES

(UNIT 17)

THE SITUATION

You are one of five audit seniors and have recently commenced working for Carregan, Walters & Co. a firm of accountants. You were employed to replace a member of staff who had left at very short notice and who had already started working on the audit of 'Diamond Dentists Ltd' for their financial year 31 March 20X9. You are now to take over the responsibility for the audit. The planning stage of the audit has just been completed, and the permanent information has been updated - this is shown on pages 148 to 149 of Appendix A and should be used to familiarise yourself with the company background and situation. You have one junior auditor, Susan Trollis assisting you on the audit who worked with the audit senior prior to his departure and is therefore familiar with the work completed during the planning.

You have been given the audit files to familiarise yourself with the client details prior to continuing the audit; (the relevant extracts are found in Appendix A).

The day after receipt of the audit file you have a meeting with the Audit Manager in charge who answers your queries, discusses the overall audit approach and outlines a number of tasks which need to be completed as part of the audit. You also inform the Audit Manager that you could not find a copy of the engagement letter on the audit file, to which he replies that he will investigate the matter.

The tasks required to be performed are outlined on pages 145 to 147 of this booklet.

TASKS TO BE COMPLETED:

Note: Prior to commencement of the tasks ensure that you familiarise yourself with the permanent audit file extract in Appendix A

Task 1

The Audit Manager has informed you that an engagement letter has not been sent to the client and therefore wishes you to prepare a draft letter for him to check and sign.

Use the headed paper on pages 155 and 156 of the answer booklet.

Task 2

At the meeting with the Audit Manager, he outlined that he is somewhat concerned at the apparent drop in standard in some of the audit files which was identified during the annual peer reviews 6 weeks ago. He is therefore considering a revision of the current training programme that exists. He asks you to prepare two memorandums for issue to all employees at Carregan, Walters & Co outlining the following:

(i)   The reasons for, and importance of quality control within the audit

(ii)   The reasons for, and importance of training audit staff, and monitoring and reviewing their performance.

Use pages 157 to 158 of the answer booklet.

Task 3

During the systems documentation stage of the audit you have prepared an ICQ to be used to assist with the audit of the wages and salaries (refer Appendix B) After giving this to Susan Trollis to complete she asks you to explain in more detail the internal control objectives being tested.

(i)   Describe the internal control objective that is being fulfilled if the controls detailed in the ICQ are in existence. Use the working paper on page 159 of the answer booklet.

(ii)   Susan has now completed the ICQ, which you have reviewed and now require her to perform the relevant testing. Prepare an audit programme which tests whether each control is operating effectively. Use pages 160 and 161 of the answer booklet.

(iii)   For each of the controls described in the ICQ explain to Susan what the consequences are for Diamond Dentists Ltd if these controls did not exist / were not operating effectively. Use page 162 of the answer booklet.

Task 4

With reference to the information contained in Appendix A in relation to the Sales system (assume that the only controls are those shown):

(i)   Complete the evaluation form on pages 163 to 165 of the answer booklet stating the weaknesses (and their implications) in the sales system and suggest recommendations for their improvement.

(ii)   Mr G Diamond has stated that he doesn't understand why a daily cash reconciliation of cash received to sales is necessary; in his opinion it is an unnecessary task which his staff can do without *(Note: this was a recommendation from last year's audit which has not yet been implemented).*

Write a letter to Mr G Diamond outlining the problems of not having a daily cash reconciliation, explain the necessity for and importance of the daily cash reconciliation; also explain the nature of such a reconciliation ie what it would comprise of. Use page 166 of the answer booklet.

(iii)   Prepare an audit programme stating which tests (including follow up checks) you would perform when performing a surprise cash count of cash sales receipts; state what date you would ideally perform the count. Use page 167 of the answer booklet.

Task 5

You are about to commence some detailed computer audit work and Susan Trollis mentioned that she has heard terms such as 'application controls' and 'general controls'; however, she has no idea what they mean.

(i)   Using the form on page 168 of the answer booklet write a memo to Susan explaining the difference between the tw o types of controls and give two examples of each type.

(ii)   Using the schedule on page 169 of the answer booklet, document the weaknesses in Diamond Dentists Ltd computer system and the effect(s) of their existence.

NOTE: You are not required to make recommendations for improvement

(iii)   Describe how you might use Computer Assisted Audit Techniques (CAATs) to test the creditor information on Diamond Dentists Ltd accounting system (you should include a description of the different types of CAAT in your answer). Use the working papers on pages 170 and 171 of the answer booklet.

Task 6

The substantive testing has now been completed and you need to conduct your overall review of the financial statements. Using the information in the profit and loss account and balance sheet in Appendix A:

(i)   Prepare notes on the working papers on pages 172 and 173 of the answer booklet explaining to Susan Trollis what the purpose of the overall review is, and,

(ii)   Using the working papers on pages 174 and 175 of the answer booklet state what checks you would perform on Diamond Dentists Ltd's profit and loss account and balance sheet; include details of the ratios you would calculate, and complete calculations for the year ended 31 March 20X9.

Task 7

With reference to the working paper extract in Appendix C detailing observations made during the test counts of the dental technician's stocks:

Prepare a management letter extract detailing the weaknesses and their implications and make recommendations in relation to stock maintenance and retention and recording of stock. Use page 176 of the answer booklet.

Task 8

Susan Trollis has asked you to explain to her what the difference is between an unqualified and qualified audit report as she thought that ideally all reports should be qualified as she thought that this indicated that the client had satisfied all necessary legislation and accounting standards. She also discusses two of the weaknesses identified during the audit with you and asks you what the audit opinion would be in each case.

(i)   Using page 177 of the answer booklet write Susan a memorandum which briefly describes the contents of an unqualified audit report

(ii)   Using the information in Appendix D (weaknesses discussed with Susan) describe the form of audit report you would give in each of the situations; use pages 178 to 179 of the answer booklet.

Task 9

The audit report has been completed and the financial statements approved by Diamond Dentists' shareholders at the AGM on 3rd July 20X9. Due to the control weaknesses in the cash sales system a qualified audit report was issued on the grounds of inherent uncertainty.

On 15th July Mr Gerry Diamond discovers that one of the receptionists had been taking money from customers and not registering the sale on the computer system. Following his investigation and police work it transpires that this fraud has been committed over the last 4 months and the total fraud amounted to £420.

Mr Gerry Diamond claims that Carregan, Walters & Co should have identified the fraud during the course of the audit and is threatening to sue for negligence.

Draft a letter Gerry Diamond for the Audit Partner to approve (using pages 180 and 181 of the answer booklet) outlining the auditor's responsibilities for detecting fraud and error in the financial statements and comment on his claim that Carregan, Walters & Co is negligent.

APPENDIX A

Permanent File Extract

HISTORY OF THE BUSINESS

Diamond Dentists Ltd has been in operation for 85 years and was started by two members of the Diamond family who subsequently passed on the business to their children.

It is currently owned by four members of the Diamond family, together with the resident Dental Technician, who has a small laboratory attached to the surgery. All five actively participate in the running of the business, and the shareholdings are as follows:

Dentist:		*Shareholding:*
MR GERRY DIAMOND	(Principal Shareholder)	30%
MRS SUE DIAMOND	(Wife of G Diamond)	20%
MISS BRENDA DIAMOND	(Sister of G Diamond)	20%
MR DAVID FLEMING	(Cousin of G Diamond)	15%
Dental Technician:		
MR TERENCE TARRANT	(Chief Dental Technician)	15%

The dentists employ four dental nurses who are 'attached' to a particular dentist and also help to provide holiday cover. Two part time receptionists are also employed who make appointments, book in patients, accept payments and follow up outstanding bills. A junior Dental Technician is also employed who works four days a week and attends a day release course. They also employ a part time accountant.

In May 20X8 they decided to computerise their systems - the system details are documented below.

COMPUTER SYSTEM DETAILS

Each Dentist has a PC in their surgery and there is one on reception; all PC's are networked, primarily to facilitate use of electronic mail and transfer of data files. There is also an additional PC in the spare surgery used by the self employed hygienist who visits once a week. The accountant also has her records on the PC used by the hygienist (who uses SAGE Accounts software), and works four mornings a week, ensuring that her visit does not coincide with the hygienist. The Chief Dental Technician also has a PC in his laboratory which is connected to the network although he does not use it extensively as he prefers the traditional manual methods which he has always used and consider that these are perfectly adequate.

Each Dentist's PC only has access to their own patient's records, whilst the reception PC can access all records. The PC in the spare surgery cannot access any patient records; the hygienist is provided with hard copy listings of patients who have booked to see her a week in advance. The PC in the Dental Laboratory also has access to all patients records - this was considered necessary to enable the technicians to confirm the work required in the absence of the relevant dentist.

There is a very basic access control required to gain entry to each PC which requires entry of a four character password which can be changed if the user decides to amend it. All Dentists decided amongst themselves to have the same password so in the event of an emergency they could access the other dentist's patients records - this password is 1234 and has not been changed since the system was implemented.

The Accountant has not yet set up a password on her PC and got her husband to remove the password control software one weekend when no-one was in as she has never used a computer before and is very nervous about using them. She is still maintaining her manual records at home as she is not convinced of the accuracy of the system.

All PCs now have internet connections (from November 20X8); however, in January 20X9 a virus infected their system which was transmitted via an email; this caused considerable disruption and had to be dealt with by a local professional computer company. Preventative measures are being considered.

ACCOUNTING SYSTEMS

Management Accounts

Management Accounts are produced by the Accountant on a monthly basis and are analysed by Dentist for the total business. The income and expenses for the Dental Technician are detailed separately. Copies of the management accounts are held on-line and are accessible by all PCs.

The Management Accounts comprise Profit and Loss A/C, Balance Sheet, Budget Report and Cash Flow statement.

Sales

Sales are primarily for cash or cheque, although acceptance of payment by delta card was introduced in January 20X9 and this is being used more extensively. It is up to the receptionist who deals with the patient to ensure that it is recorded on the computer system together with the payment method. Cheques are kept in a folder and then paid in to the bank account at the end of the week by one of the receptionists. Cash is kept in a safe box similar to the petty cash box and is paid into the bank by one of the receptionists when there seems to be a large amount in there (this is at the receptionist's discretion). The safe box is held overnight in a drawer in the reception area which is locked at night by whoever leaves the premises last – all dentists, the technician and receptionists have access to all drawers.

Sales are recorded separately for sale of products such as toothpaste, toothbrushes etc to dental fee income from check ups, dentures etc

A report is then printed on a weekly basis detailing sales for the week and passed to the Accountant.

Stock

Stock levels comprise those held by the Dental Technician and the Dentists – these are controlled entirely separately with the Technician totally responsible for his own stocks (teeth and miscellaneous denture materials). The dentists stocks are controlled by the dentists and are kept small. They comprise small low value materials used such as cotton wool, mouth rinse etc which are used for check ups. Toothpaste and toothbrushes are also held for sale to patients. The Dentists use of miscellaneous materials are updated on their PC by their dental assistant at the time of the patients appointment.

Purchases

There are twenty suppliers used by the dentists and one used by the Dental Technician. All orders for the dentists are placed by the Receptionists who review the stock levels on a weekly basis and place orders (on-line) for the appropriate amount when the established re-order level is reached. Copies of the orders are printed out at the time of placing the order and retained in an 'outstanding order' file.

The Dental Technician places orders with a rep from the firm he uses who visits every fortnight. These are on a very informal basis ie the technician verbally instructs the rep as to what he remembers he is low on and the rep writes down the order which he then telephones to the firm at the end of the week.

Payroll

The payroll is currently dealt with by a local firm of accountants who charge £150 per quarter for the service. They send a report to Diamond Dentists by the 15th of each month and it is up to the receptionist who opens the letter to pass the report to one of the dentists for them to sign a cheque for the appropriate amount. This has to be returned to the Accountants by 22nd of each month for the salaries to be paid on 28th of each month.

PROFIT & LOSS ACCOUNT Y/E

		31/3/X9		31/3/X8
		£		£
Income from Dental Fees		110,000		95,000
Income from Dental Repair Work		5,000		8,000
Cost of Dental Work		(20,000)		(18,000)
GROSS PROFIT		*85,000*		*69,000*
Staff costs	60,000		50,000	
Lease payments (premises)	5,000		5,000	
Rates	2,500		2,400	
Premises running costs	800		800	
Telephone	3,000		2,300	
Stationery	1,000		900	
Equipment hire	1,000		nil	
Postage	800		900	
Subscriptions	500		450	
TOTAL EXPENSES	*74,600*		*62750*	
Profit Before Tax		**10,400**		**6,250**
Tax		**(2,000)**		**(1,000)**
Profit After Tax		**8,400**		**5,250**

BALANCE SHEET AS AT 31/3/X9

		31/3/X9	31/3/X8

FIXED ASSETS

Fixtures and Fittings		60,000	62,000
Dental Equipment		55,000	50,000
Computer Equipment		25,000	5,000
		140,000	117,000

CURRENT ASSETS

Stock	4,000		3,000
Debtors	200		150
Prepayments	2,600		2,800
Bank current account	39,500		nil
Petty cash	900		1,200
		(47,200)	(7,150)

TOTAL ASSETS		**98,200**	**109,850**

CREDITORS: LESS THAN ONE YEAR

Trade Creditors	4,500		5,600
Bank Overdraft	nil		4,800

CREDITORS: MORE THAN ONE YEAR

Loan	25,000		

		(29,500)	**(10,400)**
NET ASSETS		**68,700**	**99,450**

CAPITAL & RESERVES

Ordinary share capital		40,000	40,000
Retained profits		28,700	59,450
		68,700	**99,450**

APPENDIX B

INTERNAL CONTROL QUESTIONNAIRE

TEST: ***Wages & Salaries***

CONTROL QUESTIONS:	YES/NO	W/P REF
1 Are formal records maintained to ensure that all hours paid for are actually worked?		
2 Does an appropriate person verify pay rates, overtime worked and gross pay calculations prior to wage payments being made?		
3 Are written notices required from an authorised individual prior to adding new employees to the payroll, and removing persons who have terminated their employment?		
4 Is authorisation required from all individuals prior to any payroll deductions (excluding statutory) being made?		
5 Are all employees required to sign for their wages prior to receiving them?		
6 Are all payroll records held in a secure area only accessible by authorised individuals?		
7 Does an appropriate official authorise pay rates?		
8 Does the accounting system ensure the complete and accurate recording of payroll costs in the financial records?		

APPENDIX C

Working Paper Extract

Discussions with the Dental Technician regarding Stock Maintenance Procedures

Note : Stock comprises false teeth used for crowns, bridges and dentures

The Dental Technician states that there is no formalised documented system used for ensuring that stock levels are maintained at a satisfactory level as he doesn't have time and the system that he's been using has always seemed to work relatively well. However, when he's very busy he has run out a few times and recently he's noticed that there seem to be large stocks of some of the teeth which he seldom uses.

The system that he's always used comprises giving the Sales Representative of the Company (Teethright Ltd) that he uses the empty base to which the teeth are attached. The Sales Rep then passes these to Teethright Ltd who send the Dental Technician the appropriate replacements, unless they don't have any in stock in which case they advise the Dental Technician of this and request that he reorders after a specified date.

On receipt of the new stocks the Dental Technician places them in drawers according to colour and size – no documented records are kept.

An invoice is sent with the stock items which the Dental Technician immediately gives to the Accountant without checking; he considers that Teethright are a reliable company and he doesn't have time to check the invoice. In his opinion, as the invoice is computerised it must be right.

Observations During Test Counts of Dental Stocks

Whilst undertaking test counts of the Dental Technician's stock of teeth you notice that he takes some loose gold from an unlocked drawer to make some gold teeth for customers. As you were not aware that stocks of gold were held and have no record of any existence of gold stocks you make enquiries and are informed that such stocks have been retained for years, but no records are held as *'there's not that much there, so it's not worth doing'*. After further consultation with an expert you ascertain its value at £1,950. However, when trying to reconcile the quantity you cannot agree it to sales and purchase invoices.

You also note that the Dental Laboratory is not locked when not in use and that a side door leading to the car park is also unlocked throughout the day even when the premised are unoccupied.

APPENDIX D

Weaknesses raised by Susan Trollis

1   Your audit tests have clearly identified that controls over cash takings are weak and you have not been able to obtain sufficient evidence to ascertain or quantify the extent of any misappropriations. You have therefore concluded from your audit tests that the financial statements could be seriously misleading and the figure for sales could be materially understated.

2   You ascertain that 3% of the value of the fixed assets held by Diamond Dentists have fallen in value by 50% since last year. However, the Directors have stated that in their opinion the fall is a temporary one and, if economic conditions change, the assets will increase in value to their book value. As such the figure for fixed assets has not been adjusted in the financial statements. However, from evidence obtained there is a high degree of uncertainty as to whether economic conditions will change and you suggest that the directors provide for a permanent diminution in value.

IMPLEMENTING AUDITING PROCEDURES

ANSWER BOOKLET

TASK 1

Carregan, Walters & Co
56 The High Street
St Maylow
Bruckingham
BN3 6HJ

TASK 1 cont'd

Carregan, Walters & Co
56 The High Street
St Maylow
Bruckingham
BN3 6HJ

TASK 2(i)

MEMORANDUM

TO:

FROM: *REF:*

DATE:

SUBJECT:

◆ FOULKS*lynch*

TASK 2(ii)

MEMORANDUM

TO:

FROM: *REF:*

DATE:

SUBJECT:

TASK 3(i)

Client: **W/P REF**:
Accounting Date:

                                                    Prepared By:
                                                    Date:
                                                    Reviewed By:
                                                    Date:

The internal control objectives being fulfilled, if the controls as outlined in the ICQ (and stated below) exist and operate effectively are as follows:

1   Are formal records maintained to ensure that all hours paid for are actually worked?
        Objective:

2   *Does an appropriate person verify pay rates, overtime worked and gross pay calculations prior to wage payments being made?*
        Objective:

3   *Are written notices required from an authorised individual prior to adding new employees to the payroll, and removing persons who have terminated their employment?*
        Objective:

4   *Is authorisation required from all individuals prior to any payroll deductions (excluding statutory) being made?*
        Objective:

5   *Are all employees required to sign for their wages prior to receiving them?*
        Objective:

6   *Are all payroll records held in a secure area only accessible by authorised individuals?*
        Objective:

7   *Does an appropriate official authorise pay rates?*
        Objective:

8   Does the accounting system ensure the complete and accurate recording of payroll costs in the financial records?
        Objective:

TASK 3(ii)

Client: **W/P REF**:
Accounting Date:

                                               Prepared By:
                                               Date:
                                               Reviewed By:
                                               Date:

AUDIT PROGRAMME

AUDIT TEST	W/P REF	WORK PERFORMED BY/DATE
Control Tested: All payroll payments are valid (for work actually performed) TESTS:		
Control Tested: Wages are correctly calculated and paid TESTS:		
Control Tested: Amounts on the payroll are for valid employees TESTS:		
Control Tested: Only authorised deductions are made TESTS:		
Control Tested: Amounts are paid to the correct individual TESTS:		

TASK 3(ii) Cont'd

AUDIT TEST	W/P REF	WORK PERFORMED BY/DATE
Control Tested: Only authorised access to records is permitted TESTS:		
Control Tested: All payroll amounts are authorised TESTS:		
Control Tested: All payroll transactions are accurately and completely recorded in the accounting records TESTS:		

TASK 3(iii)

Possible consequences if the controls did not exist/were not operating effectively:

CONTROL	*CONSEQUENCES IF NOT OPERATING EFFECTIVELY*
1 *All payroll payments are valid (for work actually performed)*	
2 *Wages are correctly calculated and paid*	
3 *Amounts on the payroll are for valid employees*	
4 *Only authorised deductions are made*	
5 *Amounts are paid to the correct individual*	
6 *Only authorised access to records is permitted*	
7 *All payroll amounts are authorised*	
8 *All payroll transactions are accurately and completely recorded in the accounting records*	

TASK 4 (i)

Client:
Accounting Date:

W/P REF:
PREPARED BY:
DATE:
REVIEWED BY:
DATE:

EVALUATION SCHEDULE

WEAKNESS	W/P REF	IMPLICATIONS	RECOMMENDATIONS

◆ FOULKS*lynch*

TASK 4 (i) cont'd

Client:
Accounting Date:

W/P REF:
PREPARED BY:
DATE:

REVIEWED BY:
DATE:

EVALUATION SCHEDULE

WEAKNESS	W/P REF	IMPLICATIONS	RECOMMENDATIONS

TASK 4 (i) cont'd

Client:
Accounting Date:

W/P REF:
PREPARED BY:
DATE:
REVIEWED BY:
DATE:

EVALUATION SCHEDULE

WEAKNESWS	W/P REF	IMPLICATIONS	RECOMMENDATIONS

◇ FOULKS*lynch*

TASK 4 (ii)

Carregan, Walters & Co
56 The High Street
St Maylow
Bruckingham
BN3 6HJ

TASK 4(iii)

Client: **W/P REF:**
Accounting Date:

Prepared By:
Date:
Reviewed By:
Date:

AUDIT PROGRAMME

AUDIT TEST	WP REF	WORK PERFORMED BY/DATE	WORK REVIEWED BY/DATE

Client: **W/P REF:**

TASK 5(i)

MEMORANDUM

TO:

FROM: *REF:*

DATE:

SUBJECT:

TASK 5(ii)

Client:
Accounting Date:

W/P REF:
PREPARED BY:
DATE:
REVIEWED BY:
DATE:

EVALUATION SCHEDULE

WEAKNESS	W/P REF	EFFECT	RECOMMENDATIONS

◆ FOULKS*lynch*

TASK 5(iii)

Client: **W/P REF:**
Accounting Date:

                                                     Prepared By:
                                                     Date:
                                                     Reviewed By:

Date:

TASK 5(iii) cont'd

Client:
Accounting Date:

W/P REF:

Prepared By:
Date:
Reviewed By:

Date:

TASK 6(i)

Client: W/P REF:
Accounting Date:

                                               Prepared By:
                                               Date:
                                               Reviewed By:
                                               Date:

TASK 6(i) cont'd

Client: **W/P REF**:
Accounting Date:

                                                     Prepared By:
                                                     Date:
                                                     Reviewed By:
                                                     Date:

◈ **FOULKS**lynch

TASK 6(ii)

Client: W/P REF:
Accounting Date:

                                               Prepared By:
                                               Date:
                                               Reviewed By:
                                               Date:

TASK 6(ii) cont'd

Client:
Accounting Date:

W/P REF:

Prepared By:
Date:
Reviewed By:
Date:

TASK 7

Carregan, Walters & Co
56 The High Street
St Maylow
Bruckingham
BN3 6HJ

TASK 8(i)

MEMORANDUM

TO:

FROM: *REF:*

DATE:

SUBJECT:

TASK 8(ii)

Client: W/P REF:
Accounting Date:

                                                   Prepared By:
                                                   Date:
                                                   Reviewed By:
                                                   Date:

Client: W/P REF:

                                                   Prepared By:
                                                   Date:
                                                   Reviewed By:
                                                   Date:

TASK 8(ii) cont'd

Client:
Accounting Date:

W/P REF:

Prepared By:
Date:
Reviewed By:
Date:

TASK 9

Carregan, Walters & Co
56 The High Street
St Maylow
Bruckingham
BN3 6HJ

TASK 9 cont'd

Carregan, Walters & Co
56 The High Street
St Maylow
Bruckingham
BN3 6HJ

ANSWERS

Chapters 1–2

FRAMEWORK OF AUDITING

1 Solution

Client:	**Foodies Ltd**	**W/P Ref:**	**XX/X**
Y/E Date:	**N/A**	**Prepared by:**	**RRT**
		Date:	**1/4/X8**
		Reviewed by:	
		Date:	

Subject: Pre-bid considerations

There are a number of factors which should be taken into consideration prior to deciding whether or not to bid for the audit of Foodies Ltd. These are as follows:

(1)   when the audit report is required to be signed;

(2)   whether staff of appropriate levels of skill and experience are available at the required times; and whether we have **sufficient** staff at the right times;

(3)   whether the firm is technically capable of auditing the enterprise, or whether specialist knowledge is required;

(4)   whether any ethical rules prohibit the firm becoming auditors of the enterprise eg, independence;

(5)   what is the scope of the audit eg, is it just a normal 'true and fair' audit or does the company wish to extend the scope to a fraud investigation?

(6)   are there any other relevant matters such as problems in past years?

(7)   the company is expanding; do we have the resources and ability to cope with their expansion?

(8)   does the company have any branches, or other sites from where they operate which may have to be visited; could we resource such visits?

2 Solution

Client:	**Foodies Ltd**	**W/P Ref:**	**A1/1**
Y/E Date:	**30 November 20X8**	**Prepared by:**	**RRT**
		Date:	**1/11/X8**
		Reviewed by:	**SLA**
		Date:	**5/11/X8**

Subject: Agenda Items

(1)   An engagement letter must be sent for the first time, defining the respective responsibilities of the client and the auditor. The precise content of the letter will depend on the client, but the basic subjects covered will generally be the same.

(2)   Background information about the enterprise must be obtained at the first audit, together with other details for the permanent file. Such information is then updated at subsequent audit visits or as details become available.

(3)   The planning of the audit approach will require particular attention in the first year. The systems and controls will need a detailed preliminary review so that the type and volume of testing required can be determined.

(4)   The comparative figures in the financial statements will have been audited by other auditors. Although the auditor is not required to express an opinion on the comparatives, he would need to be satisfied that:

(i)   the opening balance sheet and hence the current profit and loss account and cash flow statement are true and fair;

(ii)   accounting policies have been consistently applied;

(iii)   classifications in the financial statements are consistent.

Chapters 3–4

COMPANIES ACTS REQUIREMENTS

1 Solution

Task 1

To: Partners
From: Accounting Technician
Date: 1/9/X7

Subject: CA1985 provisions which strengthen auditor independence

Following investigation into the CA provisions I have outlined the main points below. If you require any further information please let me know.

The provisions of the CA85 which strengthen the independence of the auditor are as follows:

(i)   An officer or employee, or employee or partner of an officer or employee of the company is not qualified for appointment as auditor.

(ii)   The auditor has the right of access to accounting records, documents and vouchers at all times and the right to require information and explanations from officers of the company as he deems necessary.

(iii)   The auditor has the right to be heard at any general meeting on matters which concern him as auditor.

(iv)   The auditor is usually appointed by the shareholders in general meeting.

(v)   An auditor can only be removed from office by the passing of an ordinary resolution. The auditor can require written representations to be circularised to the members, and can speak at the meeting at which the resolution is to be debated.

(vi)   In any situation where the auditor ceases to hold office, he must deposit a written notice at the company's registered office which contains either a statement that there are no circumstances surrounding his resignation which should be brought to the attention of members or creditors, or a statement of such circumstances.

(vii)   A holding company auditor has a right to require information relating to subsidiary companies.

(viii) Any officer of the company who knowingly or recklessly makes a misleading, false or deceptive statement to the auditors is guilty of an offence.

(ix)   The auditor's remuneration including fees must be disclosed separately in the profit and loss account.

(x)   An auditor must be a person approved under the CA89 and be governed by the ethical standards and guidelines of a recognised supervisory body.

Task 2

Explanations to junior auditors re AAT Rules on Integrity, Objectivity and Independence

The AAT Rules of Professional Conduct are extremely important to the auditor and should be considered at all times in their work.

Integrity

This means that an accounting technician should be straightforward and honest in performing professional work.

Objectivity and Independence

This means that an accounting technician should be fair and should not allow prejudice or bias or the influence of others to override objectivity.

The requirements of the rules which specifically exist to strengthen independence are as follows:

(i) An established practice should ensure that the recurring fees from one private company (or group of clients) do not exceed 15% of the gross income of the practice.

  The limit should be restricted to 10% if the client is a public company (or a group of clients, where the holding company is a public company).

(ii) An auditor should ensure that personal relationships do not affect his objectivity. Problem areas include:

  (1) Where an auditor is giving personal tax advice to a director.
  (2) Where a partner has been involved for a long time with an audit client.
  (3) Where work is being carried out for a company dominated by an individual.

(iii) A partner in a practice or his spouse or minor child or any member of staff employed on the audit should not hold shares in the client company except in special cases (see (viii) below).

(iv) A practice should not make a loan to a client nor guarantee a client's borrowings. Neither should it accept a loan from a client or have its borrowings guaranteed by a client. This also applies to a partner in a practice or spouse or minor child.

(v) A partner or his spouse or minor child or any employee of the firm should not accept goods or services from a client on terms more favourable than those available to employees generally. Acceptance of undue hospitality can also threaten independence.

(vi) Any commissions earned should be disclosed and quantified in writing to the client.

(vii) Where a conflict of interest arises, the auditor should make full disclosure to those concerned, for example, where two clients are tendering for the same contract, or with clients in dispute. An auditor should not advise both parties and in certain situations it may be preferable to advise neither party.

(viii) Where any shares are held in an audit client company due to special cases, they should not be voted at any general meeting in any matters concerning the role of the auditor. These special cases are:

  (1) Where shares are acquired involuntarily (for example, a bequest). These should be disposed of at the earliest opportunity.

  (2) Where an Act of Parliament or the company's Articles require an auditor to hold shares - the auditor should hold the minimum necessary.

Chapter 5

AUDIT APPOINTMENT

1 Solution

Task 1

Client:	**Bentfasteners Ltd**	**W/P Ref:**	**A1/1**
Y/E Date:	**N/A**	**Prepared by:**	**RRT**
		Date:	**3/12/X7**
		Reviewed by:	**SLA**
		Date:	**15/12/X7**

Subject: **Meeting Discussion Points** - Auditors Rights Under CA85 in respect of Dismissal by Clients

The directors do not have the right to dismiss the auditors of a company; it is therefore assumed that the directors are acting in their capacity as shareholders when they indicate that they wish to appoint another firm of auditors.

The removal of the auditor is normally carried out at the AGM by simply proposing the appointment of another auditor. However, an auditor can be removed at any time by convening a general meeting. The rights of the auditor in these situations are as follows:

(i) The auditor has the right to receive a copy of the notice requesting that the existing auditor be removed. This notice must reach the company 28 days before the meeting at which the removal of the auditor is to be discussed.

(ii) The auditor has the right to make written representations to the members on matters concerning his removal, and the company must either:

- send these representations out with the notice of the meeting where the resolution is proposed to remove the auditor; or

- send these representations out separately; or

- have these representations read out at the meeting.

The company can petition the court to stop the representations being sent out or read out if they are defamatory, or the auditor is trying to gain needless publicity. The court will decide on this matter.

(iii) The auditor has the right to attend and speak at the meeting:

- where the resolution is proposed to remove him from office; and

- where his term of office would otherwise have ended, had he not been removed.

Task 2

Kirk & Co.
Certified Accountants
1071 Enterprise Road
Leicester

Pickard & Co
Certified Accountants
17 Docklands Crescent
Market Harborough
Leics.

14 January 20X0

Dear Sirs

We refer to your letter regarding your proposed appointment as auditors of Bentfasteners Ltd. In respect of this matter we would draw your attention to the following matters:

(i)   We have received verbal information from the directors of the company that they wish to remove us from office over a disagreement concerning the valuation of obsolete stock. We issued a qualified audit report, which we consider we were justified in doing, on this matter, which the directors did not agree with.

(ii)   The directors also informed us that they would ask a local firm to accept appointment because they would be more likely to accept the accounting policies of the directors.

(iii)   In view of the above comments, we have reservations concerning the integrity of the directors of this company.

If you require any further information, please contact us again so that a meeting can be arranged.

Yours faithfully

L McCoy
Partner

Task 3

To: Junior Auditor
From: Audit Senior
Date: 30/11/X7

Subject: Ethical implications for the nominee auditor if he decides to accept appointment

The ethical implications of the nominee auditor accepting Bentfasteners as a client would include:

(i)   **Independence**

      The auditor must be able to maintain his independence. It is a fundamental ethical principle that auditors must always be aware of and act upon any factors that might impair their independence. As the directors appear to be trying to influence the auditors into agreeing with the directors' interpretation of accounting principles, the proposed auditors must ensure that they do not break the principle of independence.

(ii)   **Auditors being removed**

The auditors who have been removed may consider that the new firm of auditors were incorrect to accept appointment. The outgoing firm has the right to take the matter to the Investigation and Disciplinary committee of the Association, to discuss the matter further. The new firm of auditors must be prepared to explain, before this committee, why they accepted the appointment to be auditors of Bentfasteners.

The outcome of the committee hearing could go either way, as accountants can have different views on the same matter. What is important for both the outgoing auditors and the new auditors, is that they can both show correct interpretation of the ethical guidelines of the Association.

(iii)   **Business case**

The new auditor must ensure that Bentfasteners is a client whom he would like in his client portfolio. If it is perceived by the local business community that the new auditor has in any way compromised his ethical standing by auditing this company, then this could have an adverse effect on his local client base.

Chapter 6

PLANNING THE AUDIT

1 Solution

Risks of misstatement	*Action to be taken*
Fixed asset additions	
• Two fixed assets have been recorded as one figure. The assets may have very different useful lives.	• Investigate whether the costs have been individually identified for the purpose of the depreciation calculations.
• The moulding machine may have a short life.	• Investigate the useful life of the moulding machine. Consider whether it can be adapted in the future to deal with changes in technology.
	• Take notice of repairs, costs and regularity of breakdown.
• Currency exchange loss or gain could be incorrectly accounted for on assets with deferred payment dates.	• Agree terms of payment to original contract.
The assets should be capitalised according to the rate of exchange ruling at the 1 March 20X2 and any gain or loss written off to the profit and loss account.	• Obtain a list of exchange rates and verify calculation of currency loss or gain across the 60 day payment period.
• Too much employee wage costs could be incorrectly capitalised as the conveyor fixed asset.	• Obtain schedule of conveyor costs. Check that only relevant items are included.
	• Support wage costs by timesheet details.
• The allocation of overheads to the self-constructed asset needs confirmation.	• Check for absorption of overheads at a realistic rate.
	• Compare conveyor costs to market price of similar product.
	• Scrutinise gross profit for unexplained increase.
	• Obtain directors representations in respect of the allocation of costs.
• The conveyor may have a short useful life if the quality is not good. There is a risk of under depreciating the asset.	• Establish what experience the employees have in building such an asset.

	• Look at evidence of continuous breakdowns.
	• Physically inspect the asset to ensure in working order.
• Risk that components acquired have also been included as trading stock.	• Obtain list of components required for the conveyor. Agree to the schedule of fixed asset additions.
	• Ensure no evidence of such items in the closing stock list.
• The grant could be incorrectly accounted for ie, non-compliance with SSAP 4.	• As the grant has been approved but not paid yet a debtor and deferred income account could be created in the balance sheet.
	• Check that the cash was received after date
	• Establish whether an amount of deferred income has been written off to the profit and loss account in accordance with the useful life of the assets, matching the depreciation charge.
	• Determine whether there are any claw back provisions attached to the grant.
	• Obtain a copy of the approval notice together with grant application report and review for agreement of amounts due.
	• Check that the accounting policy adopted has been correctly disclosed in the financial statements.

2   Solution

(Tutorial note: there is more to this question than meets the eye. You have to be careful to restrict your discussion to stock quantity problems rather than valuation. In addition the uncertainty in relation to opening figures may have been missed.

Task 1 had two requirements and so a columnar layout may be the most time efficient approach.*)*

Task 1

Potential risks	Action
• Different grades of coal exist. They need to be identified and sorted for accurate counting.	• Review client's stock taking instructions. • Consider problems experienced in previous years. • At start of count review site with senior official to identify types. • Liaise with surveyor.
• Goods in transit at year end or held in storage at a nearby port.	• Circularise suppliers at the year end. • Review suppliers statement reconciliations. • Enquire about levels of stock on 3rd party premises or at ports and arrange for stockholding certificate requests to be sent.
• No continuous stock records to provide support for physical quantities noted as counted.	• Attend year end count. • Observe efficiency and reasonableness of count. • Carry out test calculations and agree to stock count sheets. • Request a pile (volume) of coal be weighed to provide evidence of reasonableness of volume calculations.
• Accuracy of stock movements during the year is dependent upon correct working of weighbridge.	• Establish how often weighbridge is calibrated. • From records of goods in and despatches plus opening stock establish theoretical stock balance and compare to actual count.
• Stock belonging to 3rd parties is held at client's premises and may incorrectly be included in year end count.	• Circularise customers at year end to establish any 3rd party stock holdings. • Carry out sales cut-off tests.

- Specialist surveyor employed to count stock.
  This could give rise to problem if:

- surveyor not independent, or

- not competent ie, inaccurate assessment of volume and calculations, grades of coal mixed up.

- Business to continue whilst stock being counted, therefore, double counting could occur.

- Consider prior years problems.

- Review instructions issued to surveyor

- Consider specialist's experience and independence.

- Observe count and carry out test calculations.

- Review client's stock taking instructions for dealing with goods in and out during the Saturday. New deliveries should be kept to one side of yard and counted last. Proposed despatches should be sorted the night before and put aside. Any remaining stock not despatched to be counted at the end of the Saturday.

- Stock once counted should be allocated a stock card, such a card to be updated during the day for stock movements.

- Ensure staff attending the count note details of last goods in and out. This information can then be used in a stock movement reconciliation to support physical count total.

Task 2

Although audit evidence by the specialist surveyor is seen to be more reliable than that internally generated, ultimately test calculations performed by the auditor followed through to final stock sheets provide the most reliable substantive audit evidence.

In addition the auditor should not rely upon the work of the specialist without assessing his competence.

The auditor also needs to be aware of any cut off problems or high levels of wastage that could ultimately affect valuation.

Chapters 7–8

INTERNAL CONTROLS AND AUDIT TESTING

1   Solution

Task 1

| Client: | Burnden Ltd | W/P Ref: | F1/2 |
| Y/E Date: | 31/12/X8 | | |

Prepared by: RRT
Date: 1/5/X8
Reviewed by: GL
Date: 5/5/X8

WEAKNESS	EFFECT	RECOMMENDATIONS
The wages clerks appear to amend pay rates without any authorisation.	Unauthorised changes could occur resulting in incorrect salary payments.	Changes in rates of pay should be authorised in writing by an official outside the wages department.
There are two wages clerks dealing with the production payroll.	There is too much reliance on individual employees; at present if one is absent those duties cannot be performed by the other.	To improve control within the wages department, the duties of these clerks should be rotated during the year. Neither of the clerks should be responsible for all the functions in the department.
Personnel records are not currently maintained for individual employees.	These records are essential and at present could not be recreated in the event of failure/corruption of the computer system.	Personnel records should be kept for each employee giving details of engagement, retirement, dismissal or resignation, rates of pay, holidays etc. with a specimen signature for the employee.
The production manager verbally notifies the wages department of new employees.	As the production manager also controls the unused clock cards and pays out the wages, fictitious employees could be introduced undetected.	There should be written authorisation from the chief accountant for the appointment and removal of all employees. Unused clock cards should be kept in a secure place by someone other than the production manager. They should be issued weekly by a responsible official.
The Payroll is not currently 'authorised' by a senior employee.	Errors could exist and these would not be detected.	The Payroll should be signed by the person preparing it and then authorised by the Assistant Accountant prior to the director signing the wages cheque. Prior to authorisation, the Assistant Accountant should carry out random checks on rates of pay, amendments, etc.

Overtime is not currently authorised.	Unauthorised and incorrect overtime payments could be made.	All overtime should be authorised by the Production Manager.
Access to the computer payroll system is not restricted.	Unauthorised amendments could be made, and access could be gained to confidential information thus breaching the Data Protection Act 1998.	Access should be controlled by regularly changed unique passwords.
Clocking in and out procedures are not supervised.	Employees could be paid for work not done if fraudulent use of clock cards occurred.	Supervision of cards and timing devices should take place.
The Production Manager pays out wages alone.	Misappropriation of cash payments could occur.	Controls could be improved by having two wages clerks paying out wages. Each employee should also sign for their wages after providing identification; no employee should be permitted to take another's wages without written authorisation.
Salary increases are not currently notified in writing.	Unauthorised increases could be made.	All increases should be notified in writing by the Chief Accountant after authorisation by a director.
Personnel records are not currently kept for administrative staff and appointments are authorised by the Finance Director.	Undetected errors could occur and inappropriate appointments could be made.	Personnel records should be kept as for production staff, and appointments and dismissals authorised by all directors.

Task 2 (a)

Client:	**Burnden Ltd**	W/P Ref:	**XX/X**
Y/E Date:	**31 December 20X8**	Prepared by:	**RRT**
		Date:	**28/6/X8**
		Reviewed by:	**GL**
		Date:	**3/7/X8**

Audit Programme - Tests of Control

Objective: To test the adequacy of controls within the wages and salaries system

		W/P Ref	Performed by	Reviewed by
(i)	Observe wages payout for adherence to procedures.			
(ii)	Test authorisation and control over payroll amendments eg, test increase in pay rates to authorisation, new employees to personnel records.			
(iii)	Examine evidence of checking payroll calculations.			
(iv)	Examine evidence of approval of payrolls by a responsible official.			
(v)	Examine evidence of independent checks on payrolls.			
(vi)	Test authorities for payroll deductions eg, trade union subscriptions.			
(vii)	Test controls over unclaimed wages.			

Task 2(b)

Client:	**Burnden Ltd**	W/P Ref:	**XX/X**
Y/E Date:	**31 December 20X8**	Prepared by:	**RRT**
		Date:	**28/6/X8**
		Reviewed by:	**GL**
		Date:	**3/7/X8**

Audit Programme - Substantive Tests

Objective: To ensure wages and salaries are complete and accurate

		W/P Ref	Performed by	Reviewed by
(i)	Select a sample of clock cards and agree the hours worked. A computer would be required to do this.			
(ii)	Select a sample of wages and salaries records and check the following:			
	(a) rates of pay to appropriate documentation;			
	(b) calculation of gross pay;			
	(c) calculation of statutory and non-statutory deductions;			
	(d) calculation of gross to net.			
(iii)	Check the additions on a sample of payrolls and agree the total net pay to the cash drawn or, for salaries, agree net pay to bank credit transfer form.			
(iv)	Vouch a sample of leavers and joiners in the period to the personnel records and appropriate authorisation ensuring that leavers have been removed immediately from the payroll.			
(v)	Test posting of payroll totals to nominal ledger.			
(vi)	Check that the statutory and non-statutory deductions have been paid over correctly and on time.			
(vii)	Review weekly wage totals and obtain explanations for significant variations.			

2   Solution

Task 1

Client: **Midas Mail Order**	W/P Ref: D1/1
Y/E Date: **31 December 20X7**	Prepared by: RRT
	Date: 3/1/X8
	Reviewed by: GL
	Date: 5/1/X8

Audit Programme - Tests of Control (Sales and Cash collection system)

Objective: To test the adequacy of controls in the sales and cash collection system

		W/P Ref	Performed by	Reviewed by
(i)	Check a sample of debtor balances to ensure credit limit not exceeded during year, and review system of determining credit limits for new customers and extending those of existing customers.			
(ii)	Perform a sequence check on orders and obtain explanations for any missing documents. Check that an invoice has been raised for a sample of orders.			
(iii)	For a sample of invoices, check that an order exists. Perform a sequence check on invoices, and ensure correctly posted to ledgers.			
(iv)	Check sales ledger and bank reconciliations for a number of month-ends. Attend the opening of the post, and observe the procedures employed.			

Task 2

Four objectives of an internal control system are:

(i)   to ensure that the business of the enterprise is carried on in an orderly and efficient manner;

(ii)   to ensure adherence to management policies;

(iii)   to safeguard the assets;

(iv)   to secure as far as possible the completeness and accuracy of the records.

3   Solution

FINDINGS		RECOMMENDATIONS
Employees arriving and leaving the premises are not supervised, particularly in their clocking in and out. At the end of the week clock cards are not reviewed and authorised before being processed.	Potential consequences are employee errors, such as omissions and incorrect timing of clocking in and out. There could also be deliberate irregularities such as falsification of the arrival and departure times.	Mr Lamb should review all clock cards prior to sending to the accounts department and if the hours recorded are in accordance with his expectations he should then authorise them for processing. This could be combined with his other records such as booking of hours worked to cost cards and close day to day supervision of the factory area.
The pre-prepared clock cards are not pre-numbered. There is no evidence to say that clock cards are generated from master file details.	There is a potential for employees to be omitted or duplicated as starters and leavers are not checked.	Clock cards issued should be reconciled to clock cards returned the following week to ensure completeness of records. I would recommend that the clock cards are prepared based on information stored in the master files.
There are no batch controls over the input of wages information into the micro-computer system.	This could result in employees details being either: • incorrectly entered, • entered more than once, or • being omitted.	Mrs Gooch should continue to calculate hours worked for each employee but should also prepare a pre-list for processing including the following information: • employee name • employee number • standard and overtime hours worked. Batch totals could be taken of total hours worked by all employees. A further control would be exercised through having the number of employees confirmed on the list.
There is no evidence or review of control of processed information subsequent to input.	It is possible that errors occurring through the above mentioned shortfalls in the input system will not be discovered. Or perhaps more critically that systematic errors in the computer system will not be detected.	The payroll report should be agreed by Mrs Gooch to the pre-listing. The batch controls could be exercised through the reconciliation of total hours per the report to total hours per the pre-list. She should also agree a number of employees in total on the report. Mrs Gooch should also receive a copy of the Giro list report and the pay slips. Before passing the information to the finance director she should confirm that the various reports are in agreement to her pre-list. Individual employee calculations should be checked on a sample basis to confirm the accuracy of

		the computer system.
Cheques are prepared for employees wages without review to input documentation.	Employees could be omitted from the payments list or fictitious employees included on the payment list. Considering the already noted weaknesses above it is also possible that employees could receive payment at the wrong rate.	Mr Lewis prior to signing the cheques should receive a copy of the payroll report initialed by Mrs Gooch as being in agreement with her pre-list. Bank Giro details should be confirmed to this listing prior to the cheque being prepared.
A junior accounts clerk Miss Smith has access to master file information, in particular, employee standing data.	This is potentially the most serious weakness as this information will contain details of the employees wages rate, cumulative details of pay to date, and is also, in the current system the authority to produce payment.	The computer system has a hierarchical password structure and therefore the creation of new accounts should be taken out of the hands of Miss Smith. It is suitable that Mrs Gooch only in this department has the ability to create new employee accounts or to delete accounts, on the employees departure. This control could be strengthened by further additional controls (see below).
Mr Lamb can create or delete employee records by passing information to Miss Smith without authorisation.	Employees could leave and not be removed from the system or employees listed as joining the system could in fact be fictitious. There is also the possibility of employees being removed from the system from the wrong date. I would also be concerned that the cumulative information could be incorrect ie, pay to date and that any outstanding entitlements such as holiday pay may be inaccurate.	I would recommend that Mr Lewis become involved in the system for authorising changes in the master files for employees. Mrs Gooch should be empowered to only create or delete master file records on authorisation from Mr Lewis. He should do this only once he has received appropriate documentation from Mr Lamb ie, a copy P45 or other Inland Revenue documentation. Ideally this should be signed by the employee so the various payroll records can be created. Mr Lewis should also keep master file batch totals such as number of employees, or as a hash total, total number of employee numbers contained on the master files. Through periodic review control could be exercised to ensure that no unauthorised amendments are made to this standing data.
Back up copies of data processed are not kept in a secure or fire proof place.	Important backup and confidential data, required for any data reconstruction is exposed to possible theft, unauthorised access and damage.	Back up disks should be retained outside the accounts office in a fire proof cabinet.

4   Solution

	FINDINGS		RECOMMENDATIONS
(A)	The computerised accounts system auto-matically opens up a creditor account without any responsible official authorising it.	This could lead to fictitious accounts being created or fraudulent purchase transactions.	New creditor accounts should only be opened after on-line authorisation by a senior employee.
(B)	Purchase invoices are not authorised before being posted to the purchase ledger.	This could lead to liabilities being created for incorrect or fictitious purchases.	All purchase invoices should be authorised prior to posting to the purchase ledger.
(C)	Cheques are created and sent out without authority.	These cheques could be for incorrect amounts or made payable to the wrong supplier or be payable to fictitious suppliers.	All cheques should be raised and authorised by different individuals. The authoriser should check supporting documentation prior to signing.

Chapter 9
SAMPLING

1   Solution

Task 1				
Client: **Cromwell Ltd**			**W/P Ref:**	**E1/1**
Y/E Date: **31 March 20X7**			**Prepared by:**	**RRT**
			Date:	**6/5/X7**
			Reviewed by:	**GL**
			Date:	**10/5/X7**

Audit Programme - Cash and Bank Balances

Objective: To verify the accuracy of Cash and Bank balances

		W/P Ref	Performed by	Reviewed By
(i)	**Cash balances** The audit tests on cash balances can be split between sterling and foreign exchange balances. **Sterling** • On a surprise basis, arrange to count the cash at a sample of shops. Agree that the cash plus expense vouchers total to £250. • Review expense vouchers and ensure they are all authorised and are for appropriate sundry expenses. • Review the security arrangements for cash. • Examine the subsequent reimbursement of the imprest with a paid cheque - ensure expense vouchers are cancelled 'paid'. **Foreign exchange** • Arrange to count the foreign exchange floats as close as possible to year end. • Ensure that the currencies held are those in which you would expect them to be regularly dealing. • Compare the amounts counted with recent bank debiting instructions and a bank 'foreign department' exchange note. • Confirm, by reference to a newspaper for the year end date, the conversion rates used.				

(ii)	**Bank loan**			
	• Arrange for an appropriate bank confirmation letter to be sent well before the year end.			
	• Review the bank's reply. In particular, confirm the capital outstanding, any interest accrued not yet charged, and the interest charged during the year, to the nominal ledger. Also ensure that the client has complied with any terms of the loan.			
	• Agree repayments made with direct debits on the normal banking account bank statements. Check the allocation of capital and interest on each repayment.			
	• Check that the appropriate disclosures are made: capital outstanding - 'creditors due in more than one year'. Interest charged - 'interest payable and similar charges'. Security given - in the notes to the balance sheet.			
	• Ensure charges on assets are correctly disclosed in the accounts.			

Task 2

Client:	**Cromwell Ltd**	W/P Ref:	G1/1
Y/E Date:	**31 March 20X7**	Prepared by:	RRT
		Date:	6/5/X7
		Reviewed by:	GL
		Date:	10/5/X7

Main factors which determine sample sizes when performing substantive testing

(i)   **Assurance required**

Based on an assessment of the level of inherent risk and control risk, the auditor will determine the level of detection risk he can accept consistent with the need to manage overall audit risk to an acceptable level. The level of detection risk is the converse of the assurance required from detailed substantive testing. Thus a level of assurance of say 90% will require larger samples than a level of 50%.

(ii)   **Tolerable error**

Tolerable error is the level of error within a population that can be reached and still leave the auditor with sufficient assurance about his audit objective. Whilst not the same as materiality, it is closely related to materiality - materiality is an overall measure for the financial statements as a whole, whereas tolerable error is a subset of materiality related to individual financial statement areas. As the tolerable error increases, so the sample size decreases.

(iii)   **Expected error**

Where the auditor expects a higher than normal error rate (either from past experience of this client or because the client has alerted us to this possibility) the auditor will compensate for this by increasing his sample size.

(iv)   **Extent of stratification possible**

Where the facility exists to obtain a stratified listing of a population, this enables the auditor to deliberately bias his sample towards the higher value items. In this way it is often possible to target a high proportion of the value of the population whilst examining relatively few items. Clearly, if the extent to which stratification is possible improves, the sample sizes would be expected to reduce.

Chapters 10–12

AUDIT OF STOCKS AND FIXED ASSETS

1 Solution

Task 1				
Client: Northern Supplies plc		**W/P Ref:** E1/1		
Y/E Date: 28 February 20X7		**Prepared by:** RRT		
		Date: 6/3/X7		
		Reviewed by: GL		
		Date: 10/3/X7		

Audit Programme - Purchase and Sale of computer equipment

Objective: To verify the accuracy of figures in the financial statements re purchase and sale of computer equipment

	W/P Ref	Performed by	Reviewed by
Purchase of new computer:			
(1) verify that addition was authorised by an appropriate level of personnel;			
(2) agree the cost of the computer to the invoice;			
(3) physically verify the existence of the computer;			
(4) vouch entry in fixed asset register;			
(5) check that useful life of computer used in depreciation calculations is reasonable;			
(6) check calculation of depreciation charge;			
(7) ensure that fixed asset register reconciles to the nominal ledger.			
Disposal of old computer:			
(1) vouch proceeds to cash received;			
(2) check calculation of profit/loss on disposal;			
(3) ensure disposal was authorised;			
(4) vouch removal from fixed asset register.			

Task 2

To: Audit Manager
From: Audit Senior
Date: 30/3/X7

Subject: **Audit Problems** - Verification and value of new computer

There are a number of audit problems which I think may be experienced in respect of ascertaining whether the new computer purchased by Northern Supplies plc is stated at the correct figure. These are as follows:

(i)   The figure included in fixed assets for the new computer will be cost less depreciation. The cost of the asset is a factual amount, but the depreciation charge is subjective. SSAP 12 (revised) defines depreciation as the measure of wearing out, consumption or other reduction in the useful economic life of a fixed asset, whether arising from use, effluxion of time or obsolescence through technological or market changes. The aim of charging depreciation is to allocate the cost of the asset to those periods expected to benefit from its use. The Standard goes on to state that, if there is a permanent diminution of value of an asset, it should be written down to its estimated recoverable amount and written off over the remaining useful life.

(ii)   In the case of a computer, technological change is likely to result in obsolescence before the asset is worn out. Consequently, the company may decide it is appropriate to use a shorter depreciable life and a minimal residual value.

(iii)   Whatever useful life and residual value are chosen they should be constantly under review by both the company and the auditor.

2   Solution

Task 1

Client:	**Camry Products Ltd**	W/P Ref:	B1/1
Y/E Date:	**31 March 20X9**	Prepared by:	RRT
		Date:	3/3/X9
		Reviewed by:	GL
		Date:	10/3/X9

Planning attendance at the stocktake - Considerations

The following procedures will normally be followed by the auditor during the planning stage of an attendance at stocktake:

(i)   Review prior year's working papers to gain knowledge of the client and the type of location of stock, and also to identify any problem areas encountered last year to direct additional attention to those areas this year.

(ii)   Contact client to:

(1)   obtain copy of stocktake instructions to be issued to client's staff. These should be reviewed and any potential problem areas brought to the client's attention immediately;

(2)   agree stocktake date;

(3)   confirm location of stock including any new locations and location of material quantities;

(4)   discuss internal control over stocktake;

(5)   obtain management accounts to identify large stock types if possible eg, large orders in progress.

(iii)   Book required staff to attend stocktake.

(iv)   Consider whether the internal audit department at the company can be relied upon by the external auditors. Reviewing last year's file will give some information on this.

(v)   Brief staff due to attend stocktake on material areas to investigate.

(vi)   Assess need for specialist advice if stocks are of a difficult nature, either to count or to value.

(vii)   Ensure that if there are any stocks held at third parties an appropriate confirmation letter is sent, and that staff are booked to visit the location if the stock there is material.

Task 2

Client: **Camry Products Ltd**	W/P Ref:	E1/1
Y/E Date: **31 March 20X9**	Prepared by:	RRT
	Date:	30/4/X9
	Reviewed by:	GL
	Date:	6/5/X9

Audit Programme - Stock cut off

	W/P Ref	Performed by	Reviewed by
List the last goods inwards note, the last goods outwards note along with any numbers noted as unused in numeric sequence before these. After the stocktake, normally on the final audit:			
(1) ensure that goods despatched numbers prior to the last number are excluded from stock and that those after this last number are included in stock; and			
(2) ensure that goods received numbers prior to the last number noted are included in stock and that those after this last number are excluded from stock.			

Task 3

Accountants & Co.
London
SW1 6XY

Mr. Biggs
Stores Manager
Camry Products Ltd
Newcastle
NE6 5TL

20 February X9

Dear Mr Biggs,

Further to your recent request please find detailed below those procedures which should be adopted to ensure stock items are only counted once at the company's annual stock count. These procedures are extremely important as production is scheduled to continue throughout the stocktake which increases the risk of double counting or excluding items from stock.

(i)   One individual given authority over the whole stocktake. Ensure that all employees know who this individual is and that all queries are referred back to him.

(ii)   Divide the stock into a definite number of areas and assign teams of two counters to each area. These teams should be impressed that they must count all stock in their area, and no stock from any other area.

(iii)   Issue lists to each team of the stock that they can expect to count in each area. In some cases, such as raw material stores, pre-printed sheets showing all stock lines can be issued, although in production and finished goods this is unlikely to be possible. In these cases pre-numbered sheets will be issued and the sequence agreed for completeness both before and after the count has taken place.

(iv)   As each stock item is counted it should be identified as being counted by some unique mark. The attaching of an appropriately coloured tag is one method of doing this, with different coloured tags for each location. Thus if stock does move between locations, the colour of the tag will readily identify this.

(v)   Movement of stock should be kept to a minimum. Certainly movement between production and finished goods should not be allowed, while the number of emergency requisition notes should be kept to a small number if possible. Each emergency requisition note issued should be listed by the storeman. The official responsible for the stocktake may then ensure that the stock items are not included on the store sheets as they will be included in work in progress.

(vi)   The work in progress area could be counted at the end of work for that day. This will assist the count as items in production will not be continually moving around the shop floor. If both stores and finished goods are counted by this time, then staff will be available to count work in progress in a reasonable time. Care will be needed, however, to assess correctly the state of completion of each stock line, and guidance must be given to counters on this matter. Production staff could assist by being available for, say one hour after normal work finishes in return for some bonus payment.

(vii) Goods received during the day must be kept in a separate location and counted there so as not to be double-counted within stores.

(viii) Goods despatched should be sent out with the normal documentation from the finished goods store. If the good is tagged to indicate that it has already been counted, this should be recorded on a separate sheet. The official in charge of the stocktake must ensure at the end of the count that the finished goods sheets are reviewed and these items eliminated from stock.

Yours sincerely

Audit Manager

3   Solution

Task 1

Client:	**Barnes Wholesalers Ltd**	W/P Ref:	E1/1
Y/E Date:	**31 October 20X4**	Prepared by:	RRT
		Date:	15/9/X4
		Reviewed by:	GL
		Date:	20/9/X4

Audit Programme - Sales and purchases cut off

Objective: To ensure sales and purchase items are recorded in the correct period.

	W/P Ref	Performed by	Reviewed by
1. At the date of stocktake 13th October 20X4, tests will be as follows: **Test** • For purchases cut-off, select a sample of **X** large receipts of goods before the stocktake from the goods received notes and check that they have been recorded in the book stock records as being received before the stocktake. • Select a sample of **X** large receipts of goods after the stocktake from the goods received notes and check that they have been recorded in the book stock records as being received after the stocktake. • For sales cut-off select a sample of **X** large despatches of goods before the stocktake from the despatch notes and check that they have been recorded in the book stock records as being despatched before the stocktake; and • Select a sample of **X** large despatches of goods after the stocktake from the despatch notes and check that they have been recorded in the book stock records as being despatched after the stocktake.			

2.   At year end, tests will be as follows:

(1)   For purchases cut-off the auditor will select a sample of **X** large receipts of goods before the year-end from the goods received notes and:

- check that they have been recorded in the book stock records as being received before the year-end; and

- trace the goods to the purchase invoice and check that it has either been posted to the purchase ledger before the year-end or included in purchase accruals at the year-end.

Then, select a sample of **X** large receipts of goods after the year-end from the goods received notes and check that:

- they have been recorded in the book stock records as being received after the year-end; and

- check the goods to the purchase invoice and check that they have neither been posted to the purchase ledger before the year-end nor included in the purchase accruals at the year-end.

(2)   For sales cut-off select a sample of **X** large despatches of goods before the year-end from the despatch notes and check that:

- they had been recorded in the book stock records as being despatched before the year-end; and

- trace the goods to the sales invoice and check that it has been posted to the sales ledger before the year-end.

Select a sample of **X** large despatches of goods after the year-end from the despatch notes and check that:

- they have been recorded in the book stock records as being despatched after the year-end;

• trace the goods to the sales invoice and check that it has not been posted to the sales ledger before the year-end.				

Task 2

Client:	**Barnes Wholesalers Ltd**	**W/P Ref:**	**G1/1**
Y/E Date:	**31 October 20X4**	**Prepared by:**	**RRT**
		Date:	**3/11/X4**
		Reviewed by:	**GL**
		Date:	**10/11/X4**

Stocktake Attendance - Results

The matters I checked were as follows:

1. That the staff had been briefed before the stocktake and given written stocktaking instructions. Each team of stocktakers should have been given pre-printed, pre-numbered stock sheets indicating the description and location of the fast-moving and high value stocks to be counted, together with a predetermined section of the slow-moving, and low value stocks which they are responsible for counting. The staff were considered to determine whether they were competent to identify and count the stock, but not responsible for the custody of stock ie, that they were independent from general duties in stocks.

2. That there was no movement of stock during the stocktake, as this could result in either stock being counted twice or omitted, and would cause problems with normal cut-off procedures.

3. That the low value, slow moving stocks were counted systematically. The staff counting the stock did so in pairs to ensure that errors were not made in the counting and the recording of it.

4. That slow moving, damaged and obsolete stocks were described as such on the stock sheets - this highlights stock which may have to be valued at net realisable value ie, where obsolescence provision might be needed.

5. That management performed test counts and these were compared with the actual counts. I checked that any differences were resolved, by recounting the stock; and

6. At the end of the count that the management checked that all the stock selected for the physical count has been counted, by randomly selecting items of stock and checking that they appeared on the stock sheets.

Details recorded at the stocktake

1. Last goods received note: 905

2. Last despatch note issued prior to stocktake: 322

3. Stock sheet numbers used: 1-100

4. **Problems found:**

    There appears to be a problem with obsolescence in respect of ten stock items as there has been no movement on those items since last year. This matter has been raised with the Stores Manager and will be investigated further.

5. The stocktaking standard audit checklist was completed and is shown at W/P Ref : G1/2.

Task 3

Client:	**Barnes Wholesalers Ltd**	W/P Ref:	E1/1
Y/E Date:	**31 October 20X4**	Prepared by:	RRT
		Date:	16/9/X4
		Reviewed by:	GL
		Date:	20/9/X4

Audit Programme - Verification of stock quantities at year end

Objective: To ensure the accuracy of the stock quantities used for year end valuation.

Test	W/P Ref	Performed by	Reviewed by
(i) Test check the quantities from book stock records to the quantities used in the valuation of stock. Also, the check will be performed in the reverse direction from the valuation to the book stock records. If a file containing the book stock quantities at the year-end is available, it could be checked to the amounts used in the valuation using a computer audit program. Any differences between the two quantities would be investigated.			
(ii) Check the level of adjustments to the book stock quantities at each stocktake. If the value of adjustments is small, then the book stock quantities will be more accurate than if they are large.			
(iii) Test check that items of stock have been counted at least once during a three month period, and that all large value and fast moving stock have been counted at the stocktake on the 13th October.			
(iv) Test check the level of adjustments in the November and December 20X4 stocktakes. If the level of these adjustments is large, it may indicate that the stock quantities at the year-end are materially incorrect.			
(v) Check the level of adjustments around the year-end and obtain evidence to support the adjustments.			
(vi) Check whether there are procedures for adjusting stock quantities between stocktakes when they are found to be incorrect. When significant errors in stock quantities are detected (eg, when book stock quantities become negative, or when they are positive but there is no physical stock) the company should recount the stock and correct the book stock quantities.			

4   Solution

Task 1

Client:	**Andrew Manufacturing Ltd**	**W/P Ref:**	**E1/1**
Y/E Date:	**30 September 20X4**	**Prepared by:**	**RRT**
		Date:	**16/8/X4**
		Reviewed by:	**GL**
		Date:	**21/8/X4**

Audit Programme - Fixed Assets

Objective: To verify the accuracy of the amounts stated in the financial statements for fixed assets.

	W/P Ref	Performed by	Reviewed by

Test

(i)   Obtain from the client a schedule of movements in fixed assets for the year, check the additions on the schedule, agree the totals to the amounts in the draft accounts and the closing balances to the nominal ledger.

(ii)   Check the opening balances on the schedule and in the draft accounts to:

- the closing balances in the preceding years accounts; and

- closing balances in the underlying books and records for the preceding period.

(iii)   Vouch additions to the fixed assets to purchase invoices, HP or lease agreements, and the entry in the nominal ledger. Also, check that the item has been included in the fixed asset register.

(iv)   Check disposals to supporting documentation (eg, sales invoice or cash book) and consider whether the disposal proceeds are reasonable. Check the cost and depreciation provision at the date of disposal to the fixed asset register and check that this has been properly deducted on the schedule (in (i) above) and in the nominal ledger. Check that the profit or loss on disposal of the asset has been correctly treated in the nominal ledger.

(v)   Check the additions of cost, depreciation provision and depreciation charge of the individual fixed assets in the fixed asset register to the amounts on the schedule, draft accounts and nominal ledger.

(vi)   Physically inspect a sample of fixed assets. The check should be performed from both the fixed asset register to the fixed assets (which checks that the fixed assets in the register exist) and from the fixed asset to the fixed asset register (which checks that the fixed assets which exist are included in the fixed asset register, and hence in the accounts). In verifying fixed assets, it is important to check the serial number on the item (or vehicle registration number). However, this is not possible for most fixtures and fittings, so only agreement of the description is possible. If some of the vehicles are located in other parts of the country, obtain a certificate of existence signed by the user of the vehicle (e.g. for salesmen's cars).

(vii)   Check that the depreciation rates are reasonable. If there are losses on sale of fixed assets, it is an indication that depreciation rates are inadequate. If there are profits on the sale of fixed assets or a significant proportion of the fixed assets are fully written off, then it is an indication that depreciation rates are too high. However, auditors are more likely to accept too high a depreciation rate than too low a depreciation rate, as they would argue this is a prudent approach.

The auditor would consider whether the remaining lives of the existing fixed assets are realistic by asking the company's senior management, looking at the condition of the fixed assets and considering whether any of the fixed assets may become obsolete (e.g. a depreciation rate of 10% on cost would be unrealistic for microcomputers).

(viii)   Consider whether there are any obsolete or unused fixed assets, by asking management, inspecting board and management meetings and looking at the fixed assets in the factory. Obsolete fixed assets should be written down to estimated disposal value, and the auditor would consider whether unused fixed assets will be used again - if they are unlikely to be used again, they should be treated in the same way as obsolete fixed assets. By the term 'obsolete' the auditor would mean assets which are of no more economic value to the company - a computer may be technically obsolete, but if it is still used for processing accounting data (or other tasks), it is not 'obsolete' in terms of the discussion above.

(ix)   Inspect vehicle registration documents for motor vehicles. Check them to the fixed assets register. The vehicle registration document is not a document of title, but it is good evidence of the existence of the vehicle and that the company may own it.

(x)   Inspect the deeds of the property - the latest conveyance should be in the name of the company. Also the auditor could check with the land registry that the land is registered in the company's name.

(xi)   Based on the above audit work, the auditor would then decide whether fixed assets as stated in the accounts are correct or not.

Task 2

Memorandum

To: Junior Auditor
From: Audit Senior
Date: 21 August 20X4
Re: Fixed assets register

The fixed asset register is an extremely important control in any company as it records all fixed assets owned by the company in terms of their cost and depreciation. It usually records the location of the asset and assigns each asset a unique number. These details enable the company to maintain control over their assets and assist them with their accounting procedures.

Because of their value as an internal control, fixed asset registers are used widely within audit procedures.

If Andrew Manufacturing Ltd did not maintain a fixed asset register, the problems that would be experienced by the auditor and how it would affect the audit work and audit opinion would be as follows:

(i)   Freehold land and buildings

It appears from the relatively low monetary value ascribed to freehold land and buildings that Andrew Manufacturing Ltd has only a small number of buildings to which there had been capitalised additions in the current year. Providing the client maintained working schedules of all capitalised additions to the one or two buildings that exist this should not cause problems to the auditor. The monetary additions this year are relatively insignificant at £2,500. A detailed breakdown showing the individual invoices capitalised could easily be checked against the appropriate documentation.

(ii)   Motor vehicles

Net book value for motor vehicles at the end of the year is only about £11,000 implying that the individual number of motor vehicles must be fairly limited. Again a working schedule showing the details of the handful of vehicles that exists should be sufficient to enable the auditor to check back to the vehicle registration documents, purchase, HP or lease agreements, which will give an indication of the original cost at the time of acquisition. Again because of the insignificant number of assets involved in this category this absence of a fixed asset register would not cause a major difficulty to the auditor.

(iii)   Plant and machinery

This is the area that would cause most difficulty to the auditor if the client did not maintain a fixed asset register because the number of individual items of plant and machinery may be considerable, and whereas, with freehold land and buildings and motor vehicles, the majority of the assets will have supporting evidence of title, confirmation of title for plant and machinery is going to be considerably more difficult. Physical inspection of the asset and correlation to the originating purchase documentation by means of serial numbers on plant and machinery may be the only practical way of confirming existence and ownership of individual items which may have a small monetary unit value.

Similarly, the ease with which plant and machinery may be misappropriated by the employees of the company may cause the auditor considerable difficulties if there are inadequate physical security controls in existence in relation to the plant and machinery itself.

Chapter 13

AUDIT OF DEBTORS AND CASH

1 Solution

Task 1

To: Smith Manufacturing Ltd
                   Jones Street
                   London SW1

Date: X-X-20XX

Dear Sirs,

This is not a request for payment. It is a request for confirmation of your balance with us as at 31 December 19X7 for audit purposes.

Balance owed to us at 31 December 20X7   £ ....

If you are in agreement with the above amount, please write directly to our auditors (not to us) at the following address, for which purpose a prepaid envelope is enclosed:

Accountants & Co.
Mule Street
London SW1

If you are not in agreement, please write to our auditors, explaining the breakdown of the balance you have at 31 December 20X7, for which purpose the reverse side of this letter may be used.

Thank you for your co-operation.

Yours faithfully,

D Smith
Company secretary

Balance agreed/Not agreed*

Signature .... Position .... Date ....

* Delete as applicable

Task 2

Explanations to the junior auditor

- If a reply is not received from the initial circularisation letter, a second request should be sent. If a reply is not received from this second request then the debtors should be contacted by telephone. It is important that the client's permission is obtained prior to any direct contact.

- If direct confirmation is not possible or successful, the following procedures should be used:

  (i) review cash received after the year-end to see if the balances have been cleared;

  (ii) agree individual outstanding invoices to independent evidence such as delivery notes signed by the customer;

  (iii) review credit notes issued after the year-end to ensure debtors should not be reduced;

  (iv) review make-up of debtor balance and ensure that it consists of recent invoices;

  (v) check authorisation for any unusual entries (journals, contras) in the accounts.

Task 3

Client: **Askwith Ltd** Y/E Date: **30 June X8** Audit Programme - Cut off (Debtors)		W/P Ref: **E1/1** Prepared by: **RRT** Date: **16/5/X8** Reviewed by: **GL** Date: **21/5/X8**	
	W/P Ref	**Performed by**	**Reviewed By**
(i) Agree a sample of despatch notes, from either side of the year-end, to invoices to ensure that the dates agree (details of the last despatch notes would usually be taken at the stocktake);			
(ii) review credit notes issued after the year-end and check that they do not relate to stock returned before the year-end etc;			
(iii) check that cash received has been allocated to the correct period.			

Chapter 14

AUDIT OF LIABILITIES

1 Solution

Task 1

Client:	Farrington Ltd		W/P Ref:	E1/1
Y/E Date:	31 October X5		Prepared by:	RRT
			Date:	20/10/X5
			Reviewed by:	GL
			Date:	25/10/X5

Audit Programme - Trade Creditors

		W/P Ref	Performed by	Reviewed by
(i)	Obtain a schedule of trade creditors analysed by age. Reconcile to general ledger control account and check casts.			
(ii)	Circularise a sample of creditors and fully investigate any reconciling items.			
(iii)	Perform cut-off tests between purchases and stocks.			
(iv)	Carry out analytical reviews e.g. purchases month by month, creditors' days, etc.			

Task 2

Client:	Farrington Ltd		W/P Ref:	E1/2
Y/E Date:	31 October X5		Prepared by:	RRT
			Date:	20/10/X5
			Reviewed by:	GL
			Date:	25/10/X5

Audit Programme - Sundry Accruals

		W/P Ref	Performed by	Reviewed by
(i)	Obtain schedule of year-end accruals and comparatives. Vouch to general ledger. Perform analytical review and obtain explanations for any unusual items.			
(ii)	For a sample of accruals, vouch to backing documentation e.g. invoices.			

Task 3

Client:	**Farrington Ltd**		W/P Ref:	E1/3
Y/E Date:	**31 October X5**		Prepared by:	RRT
			Date:	20/10/X5
			Reviewed by:	GL
			Date:	25/10/X5

Audit Programme - Provisions

		W/P Ref	Performed by	Reviewed by
(i)	Scrutinise board minutes, correspondence files etc, to identify any necessary provisions.			
(ii)	For each provision identified, confirm amount with supporting documentation (e.g. correspondence with solicitors for legal action, or correspondence with architects or surveyors for factory repairs).			

◈ FOULKS*lynch*

Chapter 15

COMPUTERS IN AUDIT

1 Solution

Task 1

Accountants & Co.
London
SW1 6XY

Mr. T. Simms - Director
Kola Ltd
London
SE1 2NY

6 April X8

Dear Mr Simms,

Following our recent discussions I considered it appropriate to clarify a few matters regarding our audit approach to ensure there is no misunderstanding.

I am sure you can appreciate that audit planning is always an important part of any audit, but especially so when microcomputers are used by clients. The reasons for this are as follows:

(i) **Inappropriate systems**

In many instances the introduction of a micro based system is carried out without adequate thought as to the precise requirements.

- there will probably be no formal feasibility study;

- there will have been no systems analysis;

- there will generally be no formal specification for the system.

Micro based software is generally not specific to any one type of business, and thus there is a danger that the system is inappropriate.

In this situation, there is no suggestion of the auditors having been involved in the introduction of the system, although the advice received from your friend is at least a small measure of feasibility check.

(ii) **Poor introduction**

Micros are often introduced in a fairly relaxed manner without, for instance, a proper balancing off of the manual records, or without a parallel run. In this instance the control account imbalance may well be carried forward from the old system, and without any parallel run it is difficult to establish where the fault lies.

(iii)   **Poor day to day operations**

Micro based systems are typically introduced without the rigours of staff training, operator manuals and post implementation reviews. In this instance there is no evidence of these steps having been undertaken, and again the control account problem may well be symptomatic of accounting problems.

(iv)   **Weak internal controls**

Micro based systems do not generally have internal controls:

- the micro is typically in an open office, with free access to staff

- arrangements for backing up and storage of backup tapes/discs are usually ad hoc

- controls over operators, like segregation of duties and passwords, are generally inadequate.

In the circumstances of Kola Ltd many of the above observations are apparent:

- the machine is available for all staff
- the password is unprotected
- backing up is inadequate
- no printouts of standing data amendments are obtained.

All of these features require the auditor to amend his plan so that there is a greater emphasis on substantive testing.

If you have any queries on this matter please do not hesitate to contact me.

Yours sincerely

K Janeway
Audit Partner

Task 2

Kola Ltd
Suitable Control Procedures - Accounting System

Computer based controls are often considered within two main categories: general and application.

1.   **General Controls**

(i)   General systems development controls are not really appropriate/relevant to Kola Ltd at present. If this changes, further controls can be considered at a later date.

(ii)   General administrative controls:

(a)   Division of duties

- A clear policy should be established over who has responsibility for the system (presumably Anne) and, within that, an appropriate segregation of duties between the two accounts clerks.

- Access by other employees should be effectively restricted e.g. by the use of a key for the terminal.

(b)   File controls

- Periodic printouts of standing data should be made with a clerical check.

- Back-up should be considered on a more frequent basis, with back-up tapes stored in a locked safe elsewhere in the building

- All file amendments should be accompanied by a printout.

- Copies of the operating system software should be taken and stored safely elsewhere in the building.

(c)   Operations

- Suitable manuals should be obtained/written.

- A software house should be approached and asked to provide training.

- Passwords should be established for private use only, and a secondary level of password established for use by Anne alone for the purpose of master file amendments, and month end routines.

- Anne should be encouraged to supervise any use of the computer by the clerks.

(d)   Standby arrangements

- Consideration should be given to procedures in the event of a breakdown e.g. the services of a local bureau.

- Adequate hard copy should be retained to enable reconstruction.

2.   **Application Controls**

(a)   Over input

- Check digit over stock codes.
- Range checks for stock movements and sales invoicing.
- Sequence check over despatch note and GRN numbers.

(b)   Over processing

- The use of a batch header and subsequent reconciliation to nominal ledger posting summaries.

- Transaction listings with a subsequent manual review and approval.

(c)   Over master files

- The possibility of additional passwords for certain operations e.g. account transfers.

- The retention of printouts detailing all standing data amendments.

2   Solution

Task 1

Client:	Appendex Ltd	W/P Ref:	F1/1
Y/E Date:	X/X/XX		

Prepared by: X
Date: X/X/XX
Reviewed by: Y
Date: X/X/X

1   General Controls

WEAKNESS	EFFECT	RECOMMENDATIONS
Mr Southfork appears to have made all the changes to the software, and has been the only individual to test these changes. Furthermore, he has retained the results of the testing himself. User departments do not appear to have been involved in the choice of programs or the amendments made by Mr Southfork.	This lack of checking means that Mr Southfork could have amended the programs to his benefit (eg, entering dummy purchase invoices to be paid to himself).	A proper segregation of duties should be employed regarding program amendment and testing involving all the members of the IT department. Ideally, program amendment and program testing should be performed by separate staff in the IT department.
At present there appears to be no checking of programs against master copies stored outside of the computer to ensure that no changes have been made to them.	Unauthorised changes could be made which would not be detected.	This test should be done on a regular basis, to check not only for changes made by client staff, but also to guard against the possibility of computer viruses infecting the application programs of the company.
There are no controls in place to ensure that all program changes are adequately tested and documented.	Changes could be made which do not operate accurately or efficiently. Lack of documentation does not facilitate future development.	A definite test program for checking new programs should be set up and adhered to.

2   Application Controls

WEAKNESS	EFFECT	RECOMMENDATIONS
Input appears to take place without the input clerks checking either the completeness of items sent to them for input, or the completeness and accuracy of the data actually input to the computer itself.	Input data may contain errors or data may be omitted and this would not be detected.	Some form of batch control, or check on the number of documents should be implemented to ensure the completeness and accuracy of input; such a control could be used in later processing. A series of program controls should be implemented to ensure that data input is complete and accurate.
The input clerks do not appear to check invoices etc for appropriate approval for input to the computer.	This results in the possibility of unauthorised or incorrect documents being input to the computer.	Formal authorisation controls should be implemented to prevent unauthorised/incorrect input.

WEAKNESS	EFFECT	RECOMMENDATIONS
The lack of batch controls over input does not facilitate proper controls over processing of data.	Processing errors could occur which would not be detected.	Following implementation of input controls, checking of run to run control totals should be implemented. The balances on the ledgers at the start and end of a processing run should be reconciled to the batch of documents processed during the run.
The lack of input controls does not facilitate proper control over data output.	Output errors could occur which would not be detected.	Following implementation of input controls, procedures should be established to ensure output control totals are reconciled to input control totals, thus ensuring completeness and accuracy.
Mr Southfork appears to set up master file records whenever he sees the requirement for additional records; these are not separately authorised.	Master file records could be set up for false accounts.	All master file amendments should be authorised by an appropriate official such as Mr Barnes prior to being actioned.
The server is kept in the same room as the purchasing department which means unauthorised staff have easy access to the server.	Unauthorised amendments to programs or data could be made.	The server should be kept in a separate secure room with restricted access to help prevent unauthorised amendment of the data files. To further prevent access to the computer system and data files, a series of passwords could be used.
There is no evidence of controls to prevent or detect errors during program execution.	Data corruption could occur and would not be detected.	Procedures should be implemented to ensure that any error reports are checked on a timely basis, and appropriate action taken to correct any errors.
Mr Southfork appears to be the only person involved in the installation and maintenance of systems software.	Mr Southfork could amend the systems software for his own personal benefit.	Appropriate segregation of duties should be introduced and the systems software should be regularly checked to prevent any unauthorised changes.
Program amendments have been made by Mr Southfork, although there is no record of user manuals being updated for these changes.	Unintentional errors may occur if staff are unsure as to how to properly operate the system.	All changes should be properly recorded so that all staff have a complete record of how to correctly use the system.

Task 2

| Client: | Appendex Ltd | W/P Ref: | F1/3 |
| Y/E Date: | X/X/XX | | |

Prepared by: X
Date: X/X/XX
Reviewed by: Y
Date: X/X/XX

FINDINGS		RECOMMENDATIONS
Mr Barnes has considerable control over this system. He is responsible for ordering goods, checking goods receipts notes to his orders and invoices, as well as authorising invoices and payments to suppliers.	It is possible for Mr Barnes to defraud the company by authorising invoices for payment for which goods have not been received. These invoices could even be made out in fictitious company names made up by Mr Barnes and then paid into his bank accounts.	An appropriate segregation of duties should be set up here possibly with Mr Barnes ordering goods, a second individual checking GRNs, orders and invoices and a third authorising payments to suppliers.
Orders are confirmed by telex, with apparently no formal order document being raised.	Unauthorised orders could be placed (such as for personal use).	A formal order should be raised and signed before being sent to the supplier so both Appendex Ltd and the supplier have appropriate documentation for all orders.
The stock records appear to be updated when goods are ordered, and not when they are received. In addition, stock figures are not adjusted when deliveries occur which do not meet initial order quantities.	This will make the stock records unreliable because they will not show the actual stock levels.	The stock records should be updated from the GRN.
Invoices are not serially numbered on receipt.	Invoices could be lost during processing, causing problems with suppliers if not paid on time.	Invoices should be serially numbered on receipt.
Mr Barnes manually alters purchase invoices.	Fraudulent (undetected) amendments could be made.	Any invoices in error should be highlighted with supplies and replacement invoices requested.
No record is kept of the transfer of invoices between the accounts department and the computer department.	Invoices could be lost.	Document controls eg, log of invoices transferred daily should be implemented.
Mr Southfork sets up new creditors ledger accounts without appropriate authority.	Invalid accounts could be set up and dummy invoices could be posted to the accounts.	An authorised individual such as Mr Barnes should authorise all new ledger accounts.
Mr Barnes decides which creditors should be paid and authorises rejections on the cheques payments listing.	This is a lack of internal control; errors could be made which would go undetected.	The cashiers office should perform this function.
The purchase ledger is only printed out once a month.	This will not show a complete audit trail if invoices are entered and paid in the same month.	A full listing of the ledger should be printed at least weekly.
A balance on a creditors listing is being used as justification to raise a cheque - this is insufficient evidence.	Payments may be made when not required or inappropriate.	When directors sign cheques they should be provided with the original invoice so they can check the validity of the payment.

Goods returns notes and credit notes are currently sent to Mr Barnes.	This results in an inadequate segregation of duties.	Goods returns notes and credit notes should be sent to the accounts department.
Supplier statements are not regularly checked to purchase ledger accounts to check for completeness and validity of entries.	Invalid or incorrect entries may be undetected.	Supplier statements should be regularly checked to purchase ledger accounts.

3   Solution

Client:	Appendex Ltd	W/P Ref:	F2/1
Y/E Date:	X/X/XX	Prepared by:	X
		Date:	X/X/XX
		Reviewed by:	
		Date:	

1   Supplier statements out of balance with purchase ledger - audit significance and implications

It is unusual for as many as 15 supplier statements out of 50 to be found not to agree to the relevant supplier account in the purchase ledger. This is of extreme concern; I therefore intend to:

(i)   extend the sample size of the current test;

(ii)   perform additional substantive tests on the purchase ledger balances. An example would be confirming the balances directly with the suppliers, although as supplier statements have already been obtained from the company, additional evidence gained here could be limited;

(iii)   perform additional substantive tests on the purchases system to try and highlight and quantify the noted weaknesses in the system;

(iv)   attempt to quantify the error in monetary terms;

(v)   bring the errors to the attention of management and ask them to try and reconcile the balances;

(vi)   consider whether errors in the purchase ledger are indicative of errors in other parts of the accounting system.

I am aware of the problems in the purchases system and I need to consider whether these weaknesses could have caused the errors noted here. It is likely that alteration of invoices by Mr Barnes and the lack of internal control over credit notes will have caused some of these differences.

If as a result of additional testing I am not satisfied that the purchase ledger balances are correct, then I will have to qualify the audit report using an 'except for' opinion on the grounds of uncertainty due to limitation of scope. Additional qualifications on purchases may also be required if there is still a material uncertainty in this area.

2   Destruction of purchase ledger print out - audit significance and implications

Although the purchase ledger print-outs may be superfluous to the requirements of Mr Barnes, they do form important audit evidence. A management letter point should be raised strongly recommending that the client retain these print-outs in future. Without the print-outs I cannot easily check postings to the individual purchase ledger accounts, or review the accounts for unusual entries during the year. Although the audit trail has been lost, as noted above, it may be possible to obtain alternative audit evidence as follows:

(i)   computer records of the missing print-outs may be available, and these could be printed out;

(ii)   as the computerised purchase day book files will have been retained, it is possible that audit software could be used to reconstruct the purchase ledger accounts;

(iii)   the year end supplier balances could be agreed to supplier statements. If the end of year balances are correct with no old or unreconciled items, then it is likely that the transactions during the year were correctly treated;

(iv)   the client could be asked to manually reconstruct certain supplier accounts for me to subsequently check.

Chapters 16–18

THE FINAL AUDIT

1 Solution

XYZ & Co.
Certified Accountants
1 Lord Street
Bristol

A Shore Esq,
Managing Director
Lake Foundry Ltd
Bridgewater

6 January X8

Dear Sir,

Interim Audit for the year ended 31 March 20X8

(a) In accordance with our normal practice we are writing to you concerning matters arising out of our audit of the accounting records of your company and the systems of internal control. These points were discussed with you at our meeting on 3 January 20X8.

We must stress that our tests were necessarily limited by considerations of cost and time and should not therefore be relied upon to reveal all areas of weakness that may exist. We should appreciate your comments on the weaknesses and recommendations as set out below and suggest that we arrange a meeting at a suitable future date.

(b) **Management controls**

	Weakness	**Recommendations**
(1)	The company does not produce monthly management or financial information. Without timely and accurate financial information the company will be unable to direct effectively its planned expansion.	We recommend that monthly management accounts are prepared which provide information on sales, profitability and aged debtors and creditors.
(2)	The company does not prepare budgets or cashflow forecasts against which to monitor its performance. These are important management controls enabling the company to respond to any deviations from budget and to plan its strategy for the future.	We recommend that annual profit forecasts and cash flow forecasts are produced and that the monthly management accounts are compared to these budgets so that appropriate action can be taken immediately if necessary.

(3)   The pricing policy of the company is inadequate due to the following:

- It is informal and cannot be relied upon to be adequately updated.
- Loss making products cannot easily be identified.
- The lack of financial information means that the overhead recovery rate cannot be monitored.

We recommend that a full and detailed review of the company's costing system is carried out as a matter of urgency. We should be willing to assist in this review if required.

(4)   The impending retirement of Mr W Shore from the company and the transfer of his shares to Mr A Shore may have both commercial and taxation implications.

We recommend that specialist taxation advice is sought before the transfer of shares is effected. In addition, the loss of Mr W Shore's expertise in the company must be carefully considered and, if necessary, a replacement should be appointed as soon as possible.

(c)   **Sales and debtors**

	Weakness	**Recommendations**
(1)	Sales orders are recorded only when the goods have been produced and are ready for despatch. Thus, sales could be omitted or forgotten.	All orders received should be immediately recorded on pre-numbered sales order documents and authorised by Mr A Shore. These pre-numbered documents should comprise a five part set which can be utilised as follows:

(1)   Sales order - used to initiate production.
(2)   Delivery note - kept by customer.
(3)   Delivery note - signed by customer as proof of receipt.
(4)   Sales invoice - to customer.
(5)   Sales invoice - retained in accounts department.

	Weakness	**Recommendations**
(2)	Sales invoices are not produced until the end of the month of delivery. This could delay the receipt of cash from customers and hence adversely affect the company's liquidity.	Sales invoices should be sent to customers as soon as practical after delivery.
(3)	Sales orders and invoices are not authorised. Thus errors in pricing etc, could be made or sales made to uncreditworthy customers.	All orders and invoices should be authorised by Mr A Shore.
(4)	An aged list of debtors is not prepared at the end of each month, nor is a sales ledger control account prepared. Thus, control over the sales ledger is weak and credit control and cash collection is inefficient.	We recommend that a sales ledger control account and aged list of debtors are prepared monthly so that control over debtors and cash collection can be improved.

(d)   **Purchases and creditors**

	Weakness	**Recommendations**
(1)	There is no formal procedure for the ordering and receipt of goods. Invoices which are unauthorised and for which the goods have not been received could be posted to the ledger.	We recommend that the company introduce a pre-numbered purchase order and goods received note set. Thus, all goods ordered can be formally authorised by Mr A Shore and the goods received note can be checked to the purchase invoice before it is posted to the purchase ledger.
(2)	A purchase ledger control account and aged list of creditors is not produced at the month end. Purchase ledger balances are not checked to suppliers' statements - thus, incorrect amounts could be paid.	We recommend that a purchase ledger control account and aged list of creditors are prepared monthly. Purchase ledger balances should be checked to suppliers' statements before payments are made.

We should be happy to discuss any of the above matters in more detail should you require it. Finally, we should like to take this opportunity of thanking you and your staff for your assistance during the course of our interim audit.

Yours faithfully,

2   Solution

Task 1

Lambley Properties plc
Address

A Auditor & Co
Certified Accountants
Address

XX-XX-20X3

Dear Sir,

We confirm to the best of our knowledge and belief, and having made appropriate enquiries of other directors and officials of the company, the following representations given to you in connection with your audit of the company's financial statements for the year ended 31 January 20X3:

(i)   We acknowledge as directors our responsibility for the financial statements which have been presented to you for the purpose of your audit and all the transactions undertaken by the company have been properly reflected and recorded in the accounting records. All other records and related information, including minutes of all management and shareholders' meetings, have been made available to you.

(ii)   A wholly owned subsidiary, Keyworth Builders has been incurring losses. We believe the company has a future and we expect the company to be continuing to trade at 31 January 20X4. No decisions have been made prior to 31 January 20X3 to change the level of activities of the company and thus there are no additional costs to be provided in the accounts.

(iii)   There is a claim by Eastwood Manufacturing plc for £5 million for alleged cost of rectification of a defective building. We have obtained the opinion of a chartered surveyor and independent legal advice, and these parties confirm our view that there are no grounds for the claim from Eastwood Manufacturing plc. We believe that no provision should be included in the accounts for this claim.

(iv)   The company has at no time during the year made any arrangement, transaction or agreement to provide credit facilities (including loans, quasi-loans or credit transactions) for directors nor to guarantee or provide security for such matters.

(v)   There have been no events since the balance sheet date which would necessitate revision of the figures included in the financial statements or inclusion of a note. Should further material events occur which may necessitate revision of the figures or of a note, we will advise you accordingly.

Yours faithfully

Signed on behalf of the board of directors

Task 2

Explanation to junior auditor

A letter of representation is an example of 'management' evidence. Management may be tempted to distort the financial statements e.g. to meet the expectations put on a company by shareholders or to hide their own fraudulent activities.

The auditor is unlikely to place the same amount of reliance on management evidence as on either his own or third party evidence because of the inherent bias.

However written evidence is more reliable than oral evidence. Section 392 CA85 indicates that should management give the auditor knowingly false information, they are guilty of a criminal offence. The auditor can gain some assurance over the quality of evidence because of this provision.

The auditor would be negligent if he relied solely on the letter of representation. The statements in the letter should always be supported by other corroborative evidence.

Task 3

Client:	Lambley Properties plc	W/P Ref:	E1/1
Y/E Date:	31 January X3	Prepared by:	RRT
		Date:	2/3/X3
		Reviewed by:	GL
		Date:	5/3/X3

Audit Programme - Provision (Legal Claim)

		W/P Ref	Performed by	Reviewed by
(1)	Examine correspondence with surveyor and lawyer to and from Lambley Properties to obtain relevant information.			
(2)	Consider reliability of third parties in (1) above.			
(3)	Consider qualifications and technical ability and experience of third parties in (1).			
(4)	Review other legal correspondence between Lambley Properties and lawyer to obtain information re settlements.			
(5)	Consider need for independent, third party expert opinion.			

3   Solution

Task 1

Matters to be raised at directors meeting

(1)   Turnover has increased by 73%, and gross profit has increased from 30% to 40%;

(2)   distribution costs have risen dramatically by nearly 300% whereas administrative expenses have only increased by 8%;

(3)   considerable loss made on sale of fixed assets (£2m);

(4)   the return on trade investments is very small (approx. 2%);

(5)   the stock turnover period has lengthened from 60 to 113 days;

(6)   the current ratio has risen from 1.67 to 1.82, and the quick ratio has fallen from 0.98 to 0.85;

(7)   the credit period allowed to debtors has increased from 45 to 59 days. Similarly, credit taken has increased from 41 to 88 days.

Note: Seven issues are detailed; however only four were requested for the purposes of the question.

Task 2

Directors' questionnaire

1.   Is the system for allocating costs to profit and loss headings adequate?

2.   Are management of the opinion that administrative expenses have remained fairly constant?

3.   Is it costing the company considerably more to sell and distribute its products?

4.   Is cut off accurate?

5.   Has stock counting and valuation been accurately and consistently carried out?

6.   Have all liabilities been recorded?

7.   Have the proceeds from sale of fixed assets been correctly recorded and received?

8.   Was the depreciation rate set at too low a level?

9.   Is the loss extraordinary?

10.   Has all income due been correctly recorded?

11.   Should the value of the investments be reduced to reflect a permanent diminution?

12.   Is any stock obsolete or slow-moving and, if so, have appropriate write-downs to the cost been made?

13.   Has the age and collectability of debts been prudently assessed?

14.   Has payment to creditors been delayed as a matter of policy? Is cut-off accurate?

15.   Are creditors and debtors accurately recorded?

16.   Are there short-term arrangements with the bank for maintaining overdraft facilities?

17.   Are there plans for improving liquidity in the near future?

Task 3

Response to Director - Reasons for analytical review

The auditor is required to express an opinion on the financial statements of an enterprise. Evidence is collected on each individual element in those financial statements, but they must also be reviewed as a whole to ensure that they present the correct picture, that disclosure is adequate, etc. The review can also be useful for highlighting any potential problem areas, as in the case of Birchinlee plc.

4   Solution

Task (a)

Accountants & Co.
London
SW1 6XY

The Directors
Taggart Ltd
London
SE1 5XY

2 January 20X8

Dear Sirs,

This transaction has given Taggart Ltd some cash now, in return for a repayment with interest in four years' time. The auditor will require sight of the 'sale' document, and will discuss the matter with the directors to try and determine the exact nature of the transaction.

There are two alternatives here; either the transaction is bona fide, in which case no further action is required; or the transaction is an attempt to give finance to the company in the form of a loan which will not be shown on the balance sheet. If the latter situation is true, then Taggart Ltd is involved in an 'off balance sheet financing' arrangement ie, obtaining a loan which will not be shown in the balance sheet. The auditor would require that the commercial substance of the transaction be shown in the financial statements, and not the legal form of the transaction. In this way the financial statements will show a true and fair view.

To show the commercial substance of the transaction it will be necessary to show the amount of money received as a loan on the balance sheet. The 'sale' will similarly be cancelled and the brandy placed back into stock. The interest on the loan will be calculated annually and added to the amount of the loan, having been passed through the profit and loss account. In this way the loan will be repaid without loss when it comes to term.

If Taggart Ltd did not accept this method of disclosing this 'quasi loan' then an audit qualification would be required on an 'except for' opinion, as the auditor would disagree with the accounting treatment adopted.

If you have any further questions regarding this matter please do not hesitate to contact me.

Yours faithfully,

Task (b)

Accountants & Co.
London
SW1 6XY

The Directors
Wolfworld Ltd
London
N1 5XY

2 January 20X8

Dear Sirs,

The revaluations in Wolfworld Ltd are acceptable, as is the method of calculating the amount of the depreciation charge. The directors then want to continue charging the historical cost part of the depreciation to the profit and loss account, but charge that part of depreciation relating to the revalued amount against the revaluation reserve. This will have the effect of splitting the depreciation charge. The directors' logic here is that their profit and loss account charge for depreciation will still be comparable with companies who have not revalued their fixed assets.

FRS 15 requires that all depreciation be taken to the profit and loss account. The standard considers there should be a consistency of accounting treatment between the balance sheet and profit and loss account. The actions of the directors of Wolfworld Ltd are therefore in conflict with the FRS.

We recommend that you amend your depreciation treatment. If this is not done then an 'except for' qualification will result due to the disagreement concerning the accounting treatment.

If you have any further queries regarding this matter please do not hesitate to contact me.

Yours faithfully,

Task (c)

Accountants & Co.
London
SW1 6XY

The Directors
Basnet plc
London
E1 5XY

2 January 20X8

Dear Sirs,

You appear to consider that a cash flow statement is confusing and therefore are proposing not to produce one. However, FRS1 requires all plc's to produce a cash flow statement. Your views are therefore going against generally accepted accounting practice.

If a company does not produce a cash flow statement when it is required to do so, then this is a breach of FRS 1. A cash flow statement is an integral part of a company's financial statements. The auditor must issue an 'except for' opinion for non-compliance with FRS 1.

If you have any further queries regarding this matter please do not hesitate to contact me.

Yours faithfully,

Chapters 19–20

AUDITOR'S LIABILITY AND CURRENT ISSUES

1 Solution

Task 1

> Accountants & Co.
> London
> SW1 6XY

The Finance Director
X Ltd
Broad Street
London
SE1 2YE

1 January X8

Dear Sir,

I have outlined in this letter details of who the auditor has statutory responsibility to and explained the auditors' duties. Please contact me if you have any further questions.

The auditor has a statutory duty under CA85 to report to the shareholders whether or not the accounts show a true and fair view. Under common law, the auditor has a duty to take reasonable care in the performance of his work.

In Hedley Byrne v Heller (1964) it was established that the auditor owes a duty of care to anyone with whom a 'special relationship' exists. How far liability can be extended is a matter of legal debate.

Court cases since the Hedley Byrne decision appeared to widen the auditor's liability. In JEB Fasteners v Marks Bloom and Co, the auditors who gave an unqualified opinion on misleading financial statements were found to be negligent in respect of a third party even though they had no knowledge of that third party. The decision in Caparo Industries v Dickman and others (1989) does limit this trend, when the auditors were found to be not liable to third parties, who lost money when relying on incorrect accounts.

In order to carry out his work with due skill and care, the auditor must follow best practice (Lloyd Cheyham v Littlejohn de Paula 1985). Examples of such best practice would include attendance at stocktakes, direct confirmation of bank balances, direct confirmation of debtor balances, adherence to auditing standards and guidelines, etc.

Yours faithfully,

Task 2

Report on the auditor's duty to detect fraud

Prepared by: Auditor
Date: 31/1/X8

Terms of Reference

To produce a report on the auditor's duty to detect fraud for the Finance Director, X Ltd.

Responsibility to detect fraud

The primary responsibility for the prevention and detection of fraud rests with management. The auditor's responsibility is limited to designing and evaluating his work with a view to detecting those irregularities which might impair the truth and fairness of the view given by the financial statements.

X Ltd's situation

In the case of X Ltd, the auditor has a duty to ensure that stocks are fairly presented ie, the stocks are correctly owned, valued and disclosed. Auditors should obtain sufficient, relevant and reliable evidence to support their opinion, and should carry out their work with due skill and care.

The auditors of X Ltd planned their attendance at branch stocktakes and attended the main warehouse stocktake. The work carried out by the auditors would appear, on the basis of the information given, to be adequate, assuming that it was carried out expeditiously. In the absence of further details, conclusions as to whether or not the audit was properly carried out cannot be drawn.

2   Solution

Task 1

Accountants & Co.
London
SW1 6XY

Head of Internal Audit
Hyson Hotels plc
London
SW1 6YE

1 January 20X8

Dear Sir,

Following our recent appointment, and as we will be commencing our audit shortly I felt it would be useful to inform you of the work we would expect your department to have been performing.

(a)   The scope and objectives of the internal audit department are set by management and will vary from one organisation to another. However, common areas of activity of any internal audit department will include:

   (i)   reviewing accounting systems and internal control

   (ii)   examining financial and operating information for management, including detailed testing of transactions and balances

   (iii)   reviewing the economy, efficiency and effectiveness of operations and of the functioning of non-financial controls

(iv)   reviewing the implementation of corporate policies, plans and procedures

(v)   any other special investigative procedures.

With regard to the internal auditors of Hyson Hotels plc the work that would be carried out should include:

(i)   checks on the operation of the computer system including:

- controls over input, processing and distribution of output

- controls over access to the computer and computer records

- procedures for the maintenance of back-up files and the provision of emergency facilities in the event of hardware or software failure

- appropriate separation of duties and proper training and supervision of staff.

(ii)   checks on the system for room bookings and guests' accounts including:

- procedures for recording reservations

- procedures for accounting and handling deposits received and payments in advance

- cancellations

(iii)   test checks on the day-to-day computer transactions, including:

- completeness and accuracy checks by examining accounts for each guest and comparing these receipts and entries in the cash book

- sequence checks, on pre-numbered documents, especially purchase orders and sales invoices. Investigations should be carried out for any missing documents

- checks on closing entries in guest's accounts to ensure that charges are not made to guests who have left or to new guests occupying the same room.

(iv)   checks and tests of transactions contained in returns to head office, noting:

- adjustments for inter-hotel transactions

- amounts written off for spoilage, equipment losses and damages.

(v)   checks on other accounting systems at the hotel including:

- system of accounting for income relating to meals, drinks, snacks, etc.

- with regard to the payroll system, ensuring the existence of employees, including casual staff, and ensuring that all employees' salaries truly reflect their entitlement.

- for the purchase system, authorisation of purchase orders, payments to suppliers, and ensuring the correct treatment of returns

- with regard to petty cash expenditure, ensuring that all payments are supported by duly authorised vouchers and that regular reconciliations take place.

    (vi)   special ad hoc investigations into matters such as:

- suspected fraud

- proposed acquisitions of other hotels

- improvements to existing control systems.

(b)   The factors which the external auditor should consider, and the work which he would perform to enable him to assess the extent to which he could place reliance on the work of the internal auditor would include:

    (i)   the qualifications and experience of the head of the internal audit department and his staff - this is likely to affect the quality of their work.

    (ii)   the level to which the internal auditor reports. Ideally, it should be directly to the board of directors

    (iii)   the degree of independence with which the internal auditor works, Quite obviously, the overall objective of the internal auditor will be the same as that of the hotel, and in this respect he can never be as independent as the external auditor. However, within his own area of activity he should demonstrate an objective approach.

(c)   The external auditor would be able to rely on the work of the internal audit department in the following ways:

    (i)   As the internal auditor would have recorded the system of accounting and internal control, and evaluated it, the external auditor may use the schedules produced and consider the tests carried out and the conclusions drawn. This will obviously avoid a duplication of work which should reduce costs.

        The external auditor would probably carry out some walk-through tests, but his level of testing would be greatly reduced.

    (ii)   In addition to systems verification, the external auditor may call on the internal auditor to assist in the final audit in terms of verification of assets. In respect of Hyson Hotels, this may involve verification of:

- cash balances
- stocks held
- fixed assets.

        Any co-ordination of effort must be carefully planned to ensure a wide exposure of all of the hotels.

    (iii)   The internal auditor may be able to prepare working papers for the external auditor of analysis of nominal ledger accounts.

However, the external auditor must always be aware that the responsibility of reporting on the truth and fairness of the financial statements rests with him. He should always play a dominant role in determining materiality levels, considering audit risk and evaluating areas of judgement.

Task 2

Client:	Hyson Hotels plc		W/P Ref:	E1/1
Y/E Date:	31 December X8		Prepared by:	RRT
			Date:	1/11/X8
			Reviewed by:	GL
			Date:	5/11/X8

Audit Programme - Reliance on Internal Audit

		W/P Ref	Performed by	Reviewed by
(1)	Ascertain the qualifications and experience of internal audit department staff.			
(2)	Identify the level to which the internal audit department reports (ideally this should be the Board of Directors).			
(3)	Identify the degree of independence with which the internal auditor works (the auditor should be able to demonstrate an objective approach).			
(4)	Identify the extent to which there are any limitations on the scope of the work of the internal auditor. This would involve discussions with the internal auditor to ascertain the extent of management influence over his work.			
(5)	Review the quality of the internal auditor's documentation and working papers, as these will indicate the quality of the work performed.			
(6)	Review the extent of management response to the internal auditor's recommendations. This would involve examining both the internal auditor's reports and also minutes of board meetings.			
(7)	Re-perform tests already carried out by the internal auditor to verify the accuracy of results and ultimately the conclusions drawn.			

3   Solution

NEWSLETTER ARTICLE

Auditor's Liability

1.   Who is the auditor liable to?

The auditor may be liable as follows:

(i)   under criminal law, to the Crown, for certain specific offences under the CA85;

(ii)   under the law of contract, to the company;

(iii)   under the tort of negligence to:

(1)   the members; or

(2)   third parties.

2.   When is the auditor liable to third parties?

An auditor is expected to carry out his duties with reasonable skill and care. This duty may apply to potential users of the financial statements even where they are third parties with whom the auditor has no direct contractual obligation.

The case of **Hedley Byrne & Co Ltd v Heller & Partners (1963)** established that, if negligence in the preparation or approval of financial statements can be proved and if the auditor knew or should have known that the accounts would be relied upon by a complainant third party, then an action against the auditors may succeed. The particular circumstances for an action to succeed would depend upon the existence or otherwise of a special relationship between the auditor and the third party.

In **Caparo Industries v Dickman and Touche Ross & Co (1989)** the House of Lords held that a duty of care was not owed to potential investors in a company.

3.   Possible defences against negligence

(i)   that a duty of care was not owed to the plaintiff;

(ii)   that the audit work was performed with diligence and care and in accordance with Auditing Standards and Guidelines;

(iii)   that the audit work could not reasonably have detected the fraud given its nature and the seniority of its perpetrator;

(iv)   that the fraud had commenced before the firm took over the audit and therefore material variation would not be detected by analytical review;

(v)   that the audit opinion was, in part, based upon management assurances

However, if a material fraud has been going on for a number of years, detailed testing should have revealed any irregularities. In addition, any management assurances must always be backed up by sufficient audit work.

PRACTICE DEVOLVED ASSESSMENTS

ANSWERS

TECHNICIAN STAGE

NVQ/SVQ LEVEL 4 IN ACCOUNTING

PRACTICE DEVOLVED ASSESSMENT 1

IMPLEMENTING AUDITING PROCEDURES

(UNIT 17)

Note: Where working paper references have been used in the task answers these are purely arbitrary and entered to demonstrate the necessity for ensuring all audit working papers should be clearly cross referenced. There is no significance to the references used.

Task 1 (i)

The permanent information has been updated where shown with new information shown in italics.

Client:	Spicer Cuts Ltd	**W/P REF**:	A1/1
Accounting Date:	30/9/X8		

Prepared By:	RRT
Date:	2/1/X9
Reviewed By:	GL
Date:	2/1/X9

EXTRACT FROM PERMANENT FILE

BACKGROUND INFORMATION

Spicer Cuts Ltd was formed in 1971 by Mr Neil Spicer and his wife Christine both of whom were the principal stylists. The company has expanded rapidly since then with the establishment of three further branches. Christine no longer acts as a stylist but works principally from home undertaking all personnel related tasks.

The organisation structure of the firm's head office (and principal salon) is as follows:

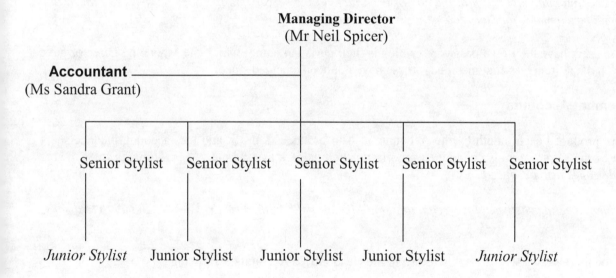

The Company Shareholders and Directors are:

Mr Neil Spicer	Managing Director	(50%)	
Mrs Christine Spicer	Personnel Director	(50%)	*Wife of Managing Director*

Mrs Spicer works primarily from home, where the personnel records are kept, and also runs the payroll each month.

None of the three other salons has a Managing Director and comprises 1 Stylist in Charge, 3 Senior Stylists and *2* Junior Stylists. The Stylist in Charge reports to the Managing Director, and all four have a meeting once a week to discuss relevant issues. In addition, Mr Neil Spicer visits each of the salons once a week on a Monday morning.

ACCOUNTING SYSTEM

Computer Environment

The salons did not have any computer facilities until August 20X7 when the Managing Director decided to invest a substantial amount of money to save time and improve management information. Prior to this all functions were totally manual.

The Head Office has two PCs, one which can be accessed by the Accountant and Managing Director and contains accounting information only. The other is used for recording stock movements, customer information (a record is held for each customer) and appointments and can be accessed by the Managing Director and any of the Stylists. The other three salons have one PC which can be accessed by the Stylist in Charge and the Senior Stylists; and are used to record stock movements and information necessary to complete the weekly returns (see next section 'Management Accounts') for Head Office. A standard software package is used for the accounting records. A separate system designed for salons (also a standard software package) is used to record stock movements etc. *All PCs (including Christine Spicer's) are now networked and weekly branch information is sent to Head Office via electronic mail.*

There is no maintenance contract in place.

The stock PC is held in the main salon area on the reception desk, whereas the Accountant's PC is in her office.

Backups are automatically taken at the end of each day via the server and the back up disks are taken to a local computer company for storage.

All of the users have their own password (which is their christian name) which the Managing Director gave them when the system was first installed – these have not been changed since.

Management Accounts

These are produced each month by the Accountant, who produces a profit and loss account, balance sheet for each of the salons and also combined reports for the business as a whole. *A cashflow forecast for the financial year is also produced.*

Management meetings between the Accountant and MD are held on the last Friday of each month to discuss results.

Each of the three salons send a weekly return to the Head Office Accountant showing:

	Monday	**Tuesday**	**Wednesday**	**Thursday**	**Friday**	**Saturday**
Cash Takings:						
Cheque Takings:						

	Stock Used:	**Stock Sold to Customers** (at 25% Mark Up)	**Stock Sold to Staff**
Shampoo			
Conditioner			
Mousse			
Hairspray			
Permanent			
Colouring			

Sales and Debtors

Sales are either by cash or cheque – the MD is currently considering accepting credit card, and debit card payments but has not yet made a decision. Cheques are usually supported by cheque card details, apart from where it is a regular customer. Any tips are put into a container and shared equally at the end of each day.

It is up to each individual stylist to record their own 'sales' on the computer system ie amount and payment method against the client name. A print out of each sale is obtained at the time of sale and these are checked to the total sales report at the end of week by the MD if he has time.

There are no debtors.

Stock

All stock items are controlled by Head Office who places all orders, using the weekly information received from each salon.

Stock sales are recorded separately to normal 'sales' using a different software package.

It is up to the individual stylist to record the sale of any stock items at the time of sale against the relevant client. All stylists at each of the salons have the ability to update the stock records.

When stock is received at Head Office, the Goods Received Note (GRN) is used to update the stock system; this is done by the MD. The MD then delivers the stock to the other three salons at his weekly visit.

A stock check is performed at the end of each quarter by the MD and the Stylists in Charge. Any discrepancies are investigated by the MD.

Staff can purchase stock items at cost price; these must be prior approved by the MD.

Purchases and Creditors

The MD, or branch Stylists in Charge review the stock levels each week and *emails* orders (using a standard order form) for replacement stock to the relevant suppliers.

When deliveries are received these are checked to the *emailed* order by the MD. The GRN is used to update the stock system and then passed to the Accountant who matches it to the invoice.

All cheques *for invoice payment* are manually written out by the Accountant and can be authorised by her (up to £500). The MD has to authorise cheques above this amount. The MD and his wife also have a business cheque book at home.

The Accountant reconciles the Purchase Ledger Control account at the end of each month to the Purchase Ledger. Purchase Ledger Accounts are also reconciled to the supplier statements when received.

Payroll

Mrs Spicer controls the payroll which is run monthly (at the end of each month) using her PC at home. She usually visits the Head Office at the end of each month to meet with the Accountant. *Payroll reports are emailed to the Accountant.*

Payment is made via bank transfer from the business account to the employees personal accounts, and Mrs Spicer faxes through the details to the bank five days prior to payment being made. Any adjustments have to then be notified to the bank within 48 hours for them to be actioned.

Any casual work is paid for in cash.

Petty Cash

A petty cash balance of £200 is held at Head Office and each of the salons. This is checked by the MD at his weekly visit who reimburses the salon with the appropriate amount. *The petty cash records are computerised and emailed to Head Office each week.*

TASK 1(ii)

Client:	Spicer Cuts Ltd		W/P REF:	B1/1
Accounting Date:	30/09/X8			
			Prepared By:	RRT
			Date:	21/1/X9
			Reviewed By:	GL
			Date:	25/1/X9

Spicer Cuts – Inherent Risks

Inherent risk is the 'susceptibility of an account balance or class of transactions to material misstatement', irrespective of related internal controls. Such risk derives from the characteristics of the entity and its environment. In simple terms it can be considered as the 'built in' risk that is associated with any organisation dependant on the type of organisation it is, the industry it operates in, the state of the market, the age of the company, number of products, number of customers etc.

The inherent risks associated with Spicer Cuts are as follows:

1   The management of the company is solely with the MD who controls all operations. Although his wife is the Personnel Director she works from home and plays little part in the actual running of the business. Likewise, the Accountant seems to be there to purely keep the accounts up to date, she does not play an active role in the financial side of the business and the management accounts produced seem somewhat limited. It is difficult to see how the business could survive without the MD even for a couple of weeks.

2   Neither the Personnel Director nor the Accountant appear to be involved in the running of the other salons at all.

3   The Stylist in Charge at one of the Salons has left and although a new one has been employed problems were experienced – this clearly demonstrated that the successful daily running of the other salons is very much dependant on the abilities of the individuals in charge.

4   The stock products are desirable and portable, yet the stock management seems a little informal, and problems have been experienced.

5   The turnover of the junior stylists is very high; although this is not a major risk, it clearly influences the abilities of the senior stylists who will have to spend an increasing amount of time training new staff members.

6   The computer system is relatively new and there appears to be very few controls, especially as regards security. There does not appear to be much experience or knowledge, nor has any training been undertaken.

TASK 2

MEMORANDUM

TO: Jane Brown

FROM: Ruth Rolfe-Tarrant   *REF:*   RRT/JB0202

DATE: 2/2/X9

SUBJECT: PERMANENT & CURRENT FILES

I understand that you seem to be somewhat confused over the distinction between permanent and current audit files, and their relevance and use within the audit.

As I have explained SAS 230 requires auditors to document all the matters which are important in supporting their audit report.

Where recurring audits are conducted for clients, working paper files are generally separated into two, namely the permanent file and the current file. These two types of file will be set up for each client. Their purpose is not the same and it is important that the correct information is held within each of the files. There should be very little duplication if at all between the two files as different information is held in each one. I have explained the differences between the two below:

Permanent File

The permanent file contains that information which is of continuing importance and is generally not specific to the financial statements of a particular period.

Typical information held within the permanent file:

• Statutory information (shareholders, directors, memorandum and articles of association etc)
• Information about the organisation (location(s), activities, organisation charts, system documentation, client contacts, bank details, solicitor details etc)
• Engagement letter
• Important agreements
• Copies of the signed accounts for each financial period

Current File

The current file contains that information which is specific to the audit of a particular period.

Typical Information held within the current file:

• Index (of working papers) for the audit
• Financial statements which are being audited
• Control schedules (partner notes, issues brought forward from previous audit, issues carried forward to next audit, budget, time record)
• Detailed audit work performed, arranged by audit area (fixed assets, debtors, stock, creditors etc)

I hope this answers your queries; if you need any further information or explanations please do not hesitate to let me know.

TASK 3

Client:	Spicer Cuts Ltd	**W/P REF**:	C1/1
Accounting Date:	30/09/X8		

Prepared By:	RRT
Date:	28/02/X9
Reviewed By:	GL
Date:	2/3/X9

INTERNAL CONTROL EVALUATION QUESTIONNAIRE

TEST: Sales System

Control Objectives: (Not required as part of answer)

Business Considerations: (Not required as part of answer)

CONTROL QUESTIONS:	COMMENTS	W/P REF
Is there reasonable assurance that :		
1 Sales are properly authorised?		
2 Sales are made to reliable payers?		
3 All goods despatched are invoiced for?		
4 All invoices are properly prepared?		
5 All invoices are properly supported by relevant documentation? Eg purchase orders		
6 All credits to customers' accounts are valid?		
7 All cash and cheques received are properly recorded and deposited on a timely basis?		
8 All outstanding invoices will be chased for payment and that bad and doubtful debts will be provided against?		
9 All transactions are properly accounted for?		
10 All cash sales are properly accounted for on a timely basis?		
11 All sundry sales are well controlled?		
12 At period end the system will accurately state debtors ie neither overstate nor understate the amount?		

TASK 3

Client:	Spicer Cuts Ltd	**W/P REF**:	C1/1
Accounting Date:	30/09/X8		
		Prepared By:	RRT
		Date:	28/02/X9
		Reviewed By:	GL
		Date:	2/3/X9

INTERNAL CONTROL EVALUATION QUESTIONNAIRE

TEST: Stock System

Control Objectives: (Not required as part of question)

Business Considerations: (Not required as part of question)

CONTROL QUESTIONS:	*COMMENTS*	*W/P REF*
Is there reasonable assurance that :		
1 Stock is safeguarded from physical loss such as theft (internal and external), fire and deterioration?		
2 Stock records are accurate and maintained up to date?		
3 The stock recorded in the accounts actually exists?		
4 All stock owned by the company is actually recorded in the accounts?		
5 The stock recorded in the accounts is actually owned by the Company (ie not by a third party)		
6 The cut off between accounting periods is accurate?		
7 The stock sheets are accurately compiled?		
8 The stock valuation is accurate, appropriate and consistent?		
9 Stock levels are reviewed to guard against obsolescence; and appropriate arrangements are made if stock becomes obsolete?		

TASK 4(i)

Client:	Spicer Cuts Ltd
Accounting Date:	30/09/X8

W/P REF:	F1/1
Prepared By:	RRT
Date:	
Reviewed By:	GL
Date:	

AUDIT PROGRAMME:

TO ENSURE THE COMPLETENESS, EXISTENCE, VALUATION & OWNERSHIP OF FIXED ASSETS

AUDIT TEST		WP REF	WORK PERFORMED BY
1	Obtain a copy of the Company's fixed asset register which shows for each asset: cost, date of purchase, depreciation and net book value		
2	Select a sample of x assets from the Company's fixed asset register and record for each item: the purchase price, purchase date, depreciation amount and method, and net book value		
3	For each sample item: physically examine the asset, and check to ensure that it is in good working order		
4	For additions in the year: check the purchase invoice to ensure that the cost has been accurately recorded in the fixed asset register, and is recorded at the correct purchase date		
5	For additions in the year: ensure that the purchase invoice has been paid in full, and that ownership has passed		
6	For disposals in the year: check that the asset is no longer being depreciated, and that any sale proceeds have been received and have been correctly accounted for.		
7	For disposals in the year check: that the profit or loss on sale has been correctly calculated and appropriately accounted for		
8	Select a sample of x fixed assets from the Company's premises and record their location, description, asset number and general condition		
9	For each sample item in '8': check that the asset is recorded in the fixed asset register and that the description and location are consistent with actual.		
10	For each sample item in '8': record the cost, purchase date, depreciation amount and method and net book value		
11	For each addition in the sample: check the relevant details to the purchase invoice, and ensure that each item is correctly recorded in the accounts		
12	Consider whether any of the assets in the sample should be written down to reflect a permanent diminution in value eg has their condition deteriorated		

TASK 4(ii)

Client:	Spicer Cuts Ltd	**W/P REF**:	F1/1
Accounting Date:	30/09/X8		
		Prepared By:	RRT
		Date:	
		Reviewed By:	GL
		Date:	

AUDIT PROGRAMME:

TO ENSURE THE ACCURACY OF THE DEPRECIATION AMOUNT IN THE FINANCIAL STATEMENTS

AUDIT TEST		WP REF	WORK PERFORMED BY
1	Select a sample of x assets from the fixed asset register and note their purchase price, date of purchase, depreciation amount and depreciation method		
2	For each sample item: check to the purchase invoice to ensure that the purchase cost has been accurately stated; and that the purchase date is correct		
3	For each sample item: check that the depreciation method used is the same as last year's; if not establish why and consider whether the change is appropriate		
4	For each sample item calculate the depreciation amount using the relevant information and check that the amount is consistent with that recorded in the fixed asset register		
5	Consider whether the recorded useful economic life of each of the sample items is appropriate		
6	For each sample item: consider whether the method used is in line with company policy and appropriate in the light of the recorded useful life of the asset		
7	For fully depreciated assets: check to ensure that they are no longer being depreciated		
8	Consider whether any of the sample items need to written down to reflect a permanent diminution in value, thereby impacting on the depreciation amount		

TASK 5

Client:	Spicer Cuts Ltd	**W/P REF**:	F1/1
Accounting Date:	30/09/X8		
		Prepared By:	RRT
		Date:	
		Reviewed By:	GL
		Date:	

Audit Review of Client's Stocktaking Instructions:

Prior to attending the client's stocktake, the stocktaking instructions should be reviewed to ensure that they appear to be adequate and facilitate control. Regard should be given to the audit guideline *'Attendance at the stocktake'* when reviewing the instructions. Points to be considered are as follows:

Do the instructions contain relevant details concerning:

1. Adequate supervision of the planning and execution of the stocktake by sufficient senior staff who are independent of the normal stocktaking procedures
2. Tidying and marking of stock items to facilitate counting of items of stock; it would be expected that the stock taking area is divided into sections for control purposes
3. The serial numbering and control of the issue and return of all the rough count records, and their retention as required by the Companies Act
4. The systematic performance of counts to ensure all stock is counted (and only counted once)
5. Ensuring that the count is conducted by at least 2 people with one counting and the other primarily checking the count, or for two independent counts to be carried out, and that any differences are investigated and resolved
6. Ensuring that stock sheets are completed in ink and are signed by those who carried out and checked the count
7. The information that should be recorded on the count records such as the location and identity of the stock items, the unit of count, the quantity counted, condition etc
8. How the production process, and stock movements are to be restricted and controlled during the count
9. How any work in progress is to be recorded (quantity, condition and stage of production) for subsequent checking with the costing and stock records
10. How the count is to be co-ordinated with cut off procedures so that documentation concerned with the flow of goods can be reconciled with the financial records (the instructions should specify that the last goods inwards and outwards notes and last internal transfer note should be recorded)
11. The reconciliation with the stock records, if any, and the identification and correction of differences

TASK 6

Client:	Spicer Cuts Ltd	**W/P REF**:	F1/1
Accounting Date:	30/09/X8		
		Prepared By:	RRT
		Date:	
		Reviewed By:	GL
		Date:	

AUDIT PROGRAMME:

TO ENSURE THAT CONTROLS ARE SUFFICIENT TO PREVENT MATERIAL FRAUD/ERROR IN THE CASH SALES SYSTEM

AUDIT TEST	WP REF	WORK PERFORMED BY
1 Select a sample of cash sales summaries for each of the salons and head office and check to: **A) TILL ROLLS** b) Paying in slips, and check the bank's date stamp and initials – verify that the daily cash takings are banked intact ie that the amount banked agrees with that banked c) Where payments are made from takings, verify the validity of such expenditure		
2 Where payments are received by post: a) Observe the procedures for opening post and check these are in line with those documented, and consider their adequacy (eg two people present; cheque log completed etc) b) Select items entered on the cheque log and trace entries to the cash book c) Paying in book		
3 From the receipts cash book select several days throughout the period and check in detail as follows: a) To entries in the cheque log, and branch returns b) With paying in slips obtained direct from the bank, observing that there is no delay in banking monies received. Check the additions of the paying in slips c) Cast and cross cast the cash book to check for accuracy d) Check postings to the sales ledger e) Check postings to the nominal ledger, including control accounts f) Check the cash book for unusual or large items and investigate		

TASK 7(i)

Client:	Spicer Cuts Ltd	**W/P REF**: E1/1	
Accounting Date:	30/9/X8		

Prepared By:	RRT
Date:	01/03/X9
Reviewed By:	GL
Date:	05/03/X9

TEST:

Reconciliation of Creditors statements to Spicer Ltd's financial statements

OBJECTIVE:

To ensure that the amount recorded for Creditors in Spicer Ltd's financial statements is accurate, and that there are no material misstatements.

TESTING PERFORMED:

A sample of 10 creditors were extracted from the Creditor's ledger and reconciled to the statements received from the suppliers.

RESULTS:

SUPPLIER	*BAL PER S'MENT*	*BAL PER S. CUTS*	*RECONCILING ITEMS*	*RECON – CILED (√)*
Split Enz Ltd	1816.78	1456.53	£360.25 – 1 invoice not included in ledger	√
Huriel Hair Products	1600.89	nil	Dispute re: total amount owing (See conclusion)	√
Conditioners & Co Ltd	1081.15	950.24	£130.91 – 1 invoice not included in ledger	√
Jazzy Dryers plc	164.25	109.50	£54.75 – 1 invoice not included in ledger	√
Solely Computers	234.23	175.00	£58.23 – 1 invoice not included in ledger	√
Sunshine Holidays	4012.59	4012.59	Agrees	√
Pete's Plumbers	910.65	850.43	£60.22 - 1 invoice not included in ledger	√
Cheapy Wholesalers	601.45	601.45	Agrees	√
Hair for your Needs	953.69	953.46	Posting error – invoice for £50.23 posted as £50.00	X
Luxury Towels Ltd	1553.99	1500.78	£53.21 – 1 invoice not included in ledger	√

CONCLUSION:

There appears to be significant problems with the timing of postings to the ledger; in essence there is a cut off problem ie invoices received prior to year end are being posted after year end.   A total amount of £717.80 in respect of such invoices needs to be added to the total amount for creditors.

In addition there was one posting error found where an invoice for £50.23 had been posted as £50.00 – although the amount is not significant, controls over the accuracy of amounts posted are weak.   The total amount for creditors needs to be increased by 23p.

An invoice related to 'Sunnie Holidays' also needs to be verified as being incurred in the normal course of business, as it appears prima facie to be for personal purposes; if this is the case then clearly it should not be included within the accounts of Spicer Cuts; creditors should be reduced by £4012.59.

There is also a significant problem with 'Huriel Hair Products' which needs to be resolved as currently this has not been included within the total amount for creditors in the financial statements as Spicer Cuts does not consider that the amount stated as due is valid.   If however, Spicer Cuts is incorrect in its assumptions, not only will the amount of £1600.89 be payable it is likely that legal costs will also be incurred; such costs would need to be provided for.   Creditors should be increased by £1600.89 until the issue is resolved.

There are a number of steps that should be taken in order to be able to verify the amount to be stated as creditors and these are summarised in 7(iii).

TASK 7(ii)

W/P REF: E1/2
PREPARED BY: RRT
DATE: X/X/XX
REVIEWED BY: GL
DATE: X/X/XX

Client: Spicer Cuts Ltd
Accounting Date: 30/09/X8

EVLUATION SCHEDULE

WEAKNESS	W/P REF	IMPLICATIONS	RECOMMENDATIONS
There appears to be a cut off problem as several invoices within the current financial year have not been included within the creditors ledger.	E1/1	The amount for creditors has been understated, thereby showing a better financial picture than is actually the case.	The true amount for creditors should be calculated and the directors advised of the amount and asked to correct the amount. The reason for the problem should be identified and this rectified.
An invoice for £4012.59 could not be found for Sunnie Holidays which is a material amount and of a transaction type not normally that incurred by a hairdressing firm.	E1/1	Transactions could be being incurred which are not in the ordinary course of the business and yet being included in the financial statements – creditors are therefore being overstated, and false accounting occurring.	A copy of the invoice should be obtained from Sunnie Holidays, and an assessment made as to whether the amount should be included in the accounts. A system of purchase orders (signed by nominated authorised individuals) should be introduced to ensure only proper amounts are included.
The amount of £1600.89 relating to Huriel Hair Products is in dispute & has not been included within the ledger and legal action is currently being threatened by ther supplier.	E1/1	If Spicer Cuts are inaccurate in their assessment they could be liable for the £1600.89 in addition to legal costs; creditors could be understated by this amount.	Discussions should be held with the Directors of Spicer Cuts and their solicitors to assess what the true situation is. Until the situation is resolved the amount should be included in creditors. (If appropriate, use of an independent legal advisor should be considered.) If Spicer Cuts are incorrect in their assessment, or if the outcome is subjective tlegal costs should be provided for.
One invoice has been posted as £50.00 rather than £50.23	E1/1	Although the amount is not material it indicates that controls (both preventative and detective) over posting accuracy are weak; and does not give comfort over the accuracy of the accounts.	A system of batch controls should be introduced to improve accuracy over posting. In addition, the creditors statements should be used as a reconciliation control each month.

FOULKS*lynch*

TASK 7(iii)

Client:	Spicer Cuts Ltd	**W/P REF**:	F1/3
Accounting Date:	30/9/X8		

Prepared By:	RRT
Date:	01/03/X9
Reviewed By:	GL
Date:	05/03/X9

Further Actions to be Taken:

1   Sunnie Holidays should be contacted and a copy invoice requested. The amount is material in the context of the Financial Statements and the purchase of a holiday is not a transaction you would normally expect a hairdressing company to undertake in the ordinary course of business.

2   Discussions should be held with Mr Neil Spicer to assess the situation with Huriel Hair Products. Proof of postage / return of goods to the supplier should also be sought from him. It should also be ascertained whether or not he has contacted his solicitors in respect of the matter and, if not, he should be advised to immediately. If there are any uncertainties regarding the outcome of the matter, then consideration should be given to contacting an independent legal adviser to obtain their view of the likely outcome. It is important that such steps are taken in order to ascertain whether or not the figure for creditors in the financial statements is correct or whether the Directors should be advised to amend the figures.

3   Invoices received and payments made after the year end should be reviewed in order to assess whether or not there are any liabilities incurred which have not been recorded in the financial statements.

4   The total creditor figure per the creditors ledger should be agreed to the purchase ledger control account to identify whether the financial records are accurate.

5   Analytical review should be performed to assess how much creditor days has changed since last year to indicate whether there are any problems not identified during normal testing.

TASK 8

Client: Spicer Cuts Ltd
Accounting Date: 30/09/X8

EVALUATION SCHEDULE

W/P REF	WEAKNESS	IMPLICATION	RECOMMENDATIONS
F1/1	There are no physical access controls; the salon PCs are situated in the main salon area. PC 1 is in the Accountant's office yet there do not appear to be any physical controls restricting access to authorised persons only.	The PCs could be damaged either accidentally (especially with the amount of hair products in use) or deliberately by vandals (who can easily see the PC from outside the shop). The high visibility also increases the risk of theft. As there is no contingency plan (refer weakness 4) this would cause considerable disruption to operations whilst new equipment was obtained.	The Salon PCs should be located in a separate room to the main salon; or an additional PC should be purchased ie using one specifically for appointments and the other for entering sales information. The room containing the 'Sales/Stock' PC, and the Accountants PC should be locked and access restricted on a needs basis. Keyboard locks should also be considered for all PCs.
F1/2	Logical access controls are weak – the password is easy to guess and there is no control forcing regular change.	Unauthorised persons could gain access to information. Information could be easily manipulated/amended.	All staff should have unique passwords which they set; they should also be issued with guidelines on choice of password. Passwords should be forced changed on a regular basis eg monthly.
F1/3	There is no maintenance/support contract in place.	If any of the PC equipment fails it could be some time before the problem is rectified, therefore causing a disruption to operations.	Disussions should be held with local Computer firms to investigate support/maintenance contract terms, and an appropriate contract taken out.
F1/4	There is no contingency plan in place.	If there was a fire, theft or loss of key staff etc then Spicer Cuts could experience a significant disruption to operations.	A contingency plan should be drafted by the MD in conjuction with the Stylists in Charge and Accountant and cover *all* aspects of the business.
F1/5	Segregation of duties is weak – stylists who undertake the work and accept the customer's payments post the information to the computer systems.	Incorrect information could easily be entered at the point of sale either deliberately ot in error; or sales may be unrecorded. Sales coulf therefore be understated.	Duties should be clearly segregated such that the stylist who undertakes the work should not enter the information onto the computer system. The possibility of employing an additional member of staff to undertake data imput should be considered.
F1/6	Staff have not received any computer training.	Staff could accidentally make errors or be unable to resolve simple problems due to their lack of knowledge and experience. Errors have already occurred yet have not yet been resolved. This could result in unnecessary costs by having to use Computer firms to resolve such issues.	Local training courses should be considered at colleges, and local computer firms who may also be able to offer on-site training.

◆ FOULKS*lynch*

TASK 9

Client:	Spicer Cuts Ltd	**W/P REF**:	F1/1
Accounting Date:	30/09/X8		
		Prepared By:	RRT
		Date:	
		Reviewed By:	GL
		Date:	

Discussion Issues – Jane Brown

As Audit Senior in charge of the audit there are a number of issues that I would be concerned about after arriving at Spicer Cuts premises. These are as follows:

1   Jane has left the Payroll report and all her working papers clearly visible to any member of staff who enters the staff room.

The Payroll system of any company clearly contains confidential information about all staff salaries, other benefits received and payments made. All companies have a duty to their staff to ensure confidentiality of such information. Jane, by leaving all relevant working papers available for anyone's access is effectively preventing the company from ensuring such a duty is maintained. In addition, audit firms have a duty of client confidentiality, which is part of their professional rules and includes keeping all working papers safe at all times. Jane has breached this rule and the client would be entitled to take action against the audit firm.

Jane should be reminded of her professional rules and the duty owed to the client, and that all audit working papers and any client information should be retained securely at all times.

2   *Jane is late to arrive at a clients*

This does not create a very professional image. The client is paying a large sum for the audit and it is therefore important for them to feel that they are getting value for money and that the job is being undertaken with professionalism and dedication.

Jane should be reminded that she must allow sufficient travelling time to cater for any traffic delays, and the importance of behaving professionally at all times.

3   *Jane has left her laptop on the desk in the staffroom with all her audit working papers on it*

There are two aspects I would raise with Jane:

(a)   The laptop is an expensive piece of equipment which is highly portable and desirable; it could therefore easily be stolen.

(b)   The laptop contains a substantial amount of confidential information on it pertaining to Spicer Cuts Ltd which could easily be accessed by any member of staff, or if an unauthorised person gained access to the premises whilst they were closed, eg overnight, such information could be passed to competitors or used for other unauthorised purposes. The audit firm (as well as Jane herself) would therefore be in breach of their duty of client confidentiality.

Jane should be instructed to keep her laptop with her at all times whilst on client premises and should not leave it unattended; she should also be reminded that when not on client premises the laptop should be retained in a secure environment at the audit firm premises or at home if there are suitable security measures in place.

4   *Jane has written her password on a post-it and attached it to the laptop*

By writing her password down Jane is facilitating access to the information on her PC to anyone even if had been turned off. This again results in a breach of client confidentiality.

I would explain to Jane the importance of logical access controls and why they are needed, and advise her never to write passwords down, or if necessary disguise them in a form not recognisable as a password such as a shopping list item or address. I would also discuss password guidelines with Jane such as typical ones to avoid ie that are easily guessable. I would ensure that she had a copy of the firm's Computer Security Guidelines.

For the remainder of the audit I would maintain close supervision over Jane to ensure that such an incident does not recur. I would also spend a couple of days with her at the clients to ensure that she understood the points discussed with her. If I was still unhappy with her performance then I would immediately raise the issue with the audit manager and discuss the possibility of another auditor being assigned to the audit in the interim whilst Jane undertook further training, and more senior supervision.

I would mention the incident to the Audit Manager anyway and suggest that Jane undertake some security training to reinforce those points discussed with her (as above) and also recommend that she work alongside another audit junior on her next audit assignment to assist her in understanding the requirements of her.

TASK 10

Management Letter Extract:

> *Heaton Brooking & Co*
> *2 Main Road*
> *Manchester*
> *MU4 6HJ*

PRIVATE AND CONFIDENTIAL

THE DIRECTORS
Spicer Cuts Ltd
The High Street
Manchester
MR6 8SQ

1 March 20X9

Dear Mr Spicer

Spicer Cuts Ltd

Audit for the year ended 30 September 20X8

In accordance with our normal practice, we are writing to you with regard to matters arising out of our audit for the year ended 30 September 20X8 which we consider should be brought to your attention.

Our responsibilities as auditors are governed by the Companies Act and principally require us to report on the accounts laid before the company in general meeting.

This report has been prepared for the sole use of the directors of Spicer Cuts Ltd. None of its contents may be disclosed to third parties without our written consent. Heaton Brooking & Co assumes no liability to any other persons.

The matters detailed in this report reflect matters coming to our attention during the course of our audit. They are not intended to be a comprehensive statement of all weaknesses that may exist or of all improvements that could be made. We set out below those matters which we consider to be of fundamental importance. Other matters of lesser significance, but which still require your attention, are dealt with in Section B.

In order to ensure a timely resolution to these problems, Heaton, Brooking & Co would be willing to assist you with any of the issues detailed below. The terms of any such assignment would be agreed separately.

Section A

(a)   ***Physical Access Controls***

There are no physical access controls; the salon PCs are situated in the main salon area.

PC 1 is in the Accountant's office yet there do not appear to be any physical controls restricting access to authorised persons only.

Implication

The PCs could be damaged either accidentally (especially with the amount of hair products in use) or deliberately by vandals (who can easily see the PC from outside the shop). The high visibility also increases the risk of theft. As there is no contingency plan (refer weakness 4) this would cause considerable disruption to operations whilst new equipment was obtained.

Recommendation

The Salon PCs should be located in a separate room to the main salon; or an additional PC should be purchased ie using one specifically for appointments and the other for entering sales information. The room containing the 'Sales/Stock' PC, and the Accountants PC should be locked and access restricted on a needs basis. Keyboard locks should also be considered for all PCs.

(b)   ***Logical Access Controls***

Logical access controls are weak – the password is easy to guess and there is no control forcing regular change.

Implication

Unauthorised persons could gain access to information. Information could be easily manipulated/amended

Recommendation

All staff should have unique passwords which they set; they should also be issued with guidelines on choice of password. Passwords should be forced changed on a regular basis eg monthly.

(c)   ***Segregation of Duties***

Segregation of duties is weak – stylists who undertake the work and accept the customer's payments post the information to the computer system.

Implication

Incorrect information could easily be entered at the point of sale either deliberately or in error; or sales may be unrecorded. Sales could therefore be understated

Recommendation

Duties should be clearly segregated such that the stylist who undertakes the work should not enter the information onto the computer system. The possibility of employing an additional member of staff to undertake data input only should be considered.

Section B

(a)   *Maintenance/Support Contract*

There is no maintenance/support contract in place.

Implication

If any of the PC equipment fails it could be some time before the problem is rectified whilst a source was found who could resolve the problem(s), therefore causing a disruption to operations. By having to use an 'emergency' solution in the event of a breakdown this could be very costly.

Recommendation

Discussions should be held with local Computer firms to investigate maintenance/support contract terms, and an appropriate contract taken out; the contract should cover both Head Office and the other salons computer facilities. A cost benefit analysis should be undertaken to ensure that the best solution is obtained.

(a)   *Contingency Plan*

There is no contingency plan in place.

Implication

If there was a fire, theft or significant member of staff left etc then Spicer Cuts could experience a significant disruption to operations whilst a solution was sought; this could in turn result in higher costs and/or expensive temporary measures having to be taken in the interim which could be avoided if an effective plan existed.

Recommendation

A contingency plan should be drafted by the MD in conjunction with the Stylists in Charge and Accountant and cover *all* aspects of the business. This should be fully 'tested' to ensure it is workable and practical. Discussions could be held with other similar firms or the local small business enterprise organisation for advice.

(c)   *Staff Training*

Staff have not received any computer training.

Implication

Staff could accidentally make errors or be unable to resolve simple problems due to their lack of knowledge and experience. Errors have already occurred and the cause of these has not yet been resolved by the accountant. In order to resolve problems unnecessary costs may be incurred by having to use computer firms to resolve such issues, especially if 'emergency' facilities have to be used rather than through a structured support contract.

Recommendation

Local training courses run by colleges and computer firms should be investigated. Local computer firms may also be able to offer on-site training at Head Office and the other salons.

If you have any queries regarding any of the points above please do not hesitate to contact us.

Yours sincerely

R Rolfe-Tarrant
Partner in Charge of Audit

◈ FOULKS*lynch*

TECHNICIAN STAGE

NVQ/SVQ LEVEL 4 IN ACCOUNTING

PRACTICE DEVOLVED ASSESSMENT 2

IMPLEMENTING AUDITING PROCEDURES

(UNIT 17)

TASK 1

Carregan, Walters & Co
56 The High Street
St Maylow
Bruckingham
BN3 6HJ

The Directors
Diamond Dentists Ltd
Zandria Road
Bruckingham
BW1 6XY

2/2/X9
Letter of Engagement

To the Directors, Diamond Dentists Ltd

The purpose of this letter is to set out the basis on which we (are to) act as auditors of Diamond Dentists Ltd and the respective responsibilities of the directors and ourselves.

Responsibilities of Directors and Auditors

As directors of Diamond Dentists Ltd, you are responsible for ensuring that the company maintains proper accounting records and for preparing financial statements which give a true and fair view and have been prepared in accordance with the Companies Act 1985. You are also responsible for making available to us, as required, all the company's accounting records and all other relevant records and related information, including minutes of all management and shareholders meetings.

We have a statutory responsibility to report to the members whether in our opinion the financial statements give a true and fair view and whether they have been properly prepared in accordance with the Companies Act 1985. In arriving at our opinion, we are required to consider the following matters, and to report on any in respect of which we are not satisfied:

- Whether proper accounting records have been maintained by Diamond Dentists Ltd

- Whether the company's balance sheet and profit and loss account are in agreement with the accounting records and returns

- Whether we have obtained all the information and explanations which we consider necessary for the purposes of our audit, and

- Whether the information given in the directors' report is consistent with the financial statements.

In addition, there are certain other matters which according to the circumstances, may need to be dealt with in our report.

We have a professional responsibility to report if the financial statements do not comply in any material respect with applicable accounting standards, unless in our opinion the non-compliance is justified in the circumstances and we would consider:

- Whether the departure is required in order for the financial statements to give a true and fair view, and

- Whether adequate disclosure has been made concerning the departure

Scope of the Audit

Our audit will be conducted in accordance with the Auditing Standards issued by the Auditing Practices Board, and will include such tests of transactions and of the existence, ownership and valuation of assets and liabilities as we consider necessary. We shall obtain an understanding of the accounting and internal control systems in order to assess their adequacy as a basis for the preparation of the financial statements and to establish whether proper accounting records have been maintained by the company. We shall expect to obtain such appropriate evidence as we consider sufficient to enable us to draw reasonable conclusions therefrom.

The nature and extent of our procedures will vary according to our assessment of the company's accounting system and, where we wish to place reliance on it, the internal control system, and may cover any aspect of the business' operations that we consider appropriate. Our audit is not designed to identify all significant weaknesses in the company's systems but if such weaknesses come to our attention, we shall report them to you.

As part of our normal audit procedures, we may request you to provide written confirmation of certain oral representations which we have received from you during the course of the audit on matters having a material effect on the financial statements.

In order to assist us with the examination of your financial statements, we shall request sight of all documents or statements, including the chairman's statements, operating and financial review and the directors' report, which are due to be issued with the financial statements. We are also entitled to attend all general meetings of the company and to receive notice of all such meetings.

The responsibility for safeguarding the assets of the company and for the prevention and detection of fraud, error and non-compliance with law or regulations rests with yourselves. However, we shall plan our audit so that we have a reasonable expectation of detecting material misstatements in the financial statements or accounting records, but our examination should not be relied upon to disclose all such material misstatements or frauds, errors or instances of non-compliance as may exist.

We shall not be treated as having notice, for the purposes of our audit responsibilities, of information provided to members of our firm other than those engaged on the audit. Once we have issued our report we have no further direct responsibility in relation to the financial statements for that financial year. However, we expect that you will inform us of any material event occurring between the date of our report and that of the Annual General Meeting which may affect the financial statements.

Fees

Our fees are computed on the basis of the time spent on your affairs by the partners and our staff and on the levels of skill and responsibility involved. Unless otherwise agreed, our fees will be billed at the completion of the audit and will be due on presentation.

Applicable Law

This letter shall be governed by and construed in accordance with English Law. The English Courts shall have exclusive jurisdiction in relation to any claim, dispute or diffe0rence concerning the engagement letter, and any matter arising from it.

Agreement of Terms

Once it has been agreed, this letter will remain effective, from one audit appointment to another, until it is replaced. Could you please confirm in writing your agreement to these terms by signing and returning the enclosed copy of this letter, or let us know if they are not in accordance with your understanding of our terms of engagement.

Yours faithfully

Audit Partner

Carregan, Walters & Co

We agree to the terms of this letter

Signed for and on behalf of Diamond Dentists Ltd

TASK 2(i)

MEMORANDUM

TO: All Employees

FROM: Ruth Rolfe-Tarrant, Audit Senior   *REF:*   RRT/CWQual1

DATE: 15/4/X9

SUBJECT: Quality Control of Audit Work

Following the completion of a number of recent audits it has been considered worthwhile reiterating some points in respect of quality control over audit work and why quality is so important. I have therefore outlined below the main issues in respect of this matter, however, if anyone has any queries or would like any further information please do not hesitate to contact me.

There is an auditing standard (SAS 240) specifically covering the issue of quality control, and concentrates on two main areas:

- policies and procedures of auditors regarding audit work generally; and
- procedures regarding the work delegated to assistants on an individual audit

All audit firms are expected to have procedures which are sufficient to ensure adherence to the requirements of the SAS in both quality control at the level of the firm and at the level of the audit

It is vital that audit work adheres to the firms quality control procedures at all times for all audits, even if it is an audit which has been performed several times before. One of the main reasons for this is that the audit file is the evidence that the audit has been competently performed in line with best practice; it clearly demonstrates that the auditor completed his work thoroughly, selected appropriate sample sizes and can justify any actions taken and/or statements made. This is important especially if the auditor has to justify his audit opinion in a court of law.

Further points which should always be adhered to are as follows:

- The standard audit file structure, as laid down by the firm should always be used
- All working papers should be initialled and dated by both the person who prepared it and the person who reviewed it (it should also detail the points outlined below).
- Any review points should always be cleared prior to the end of the audit
- Every working paper used should show:
  - the client's name
  - the balance sheet date
  - the file reference of the working paper
  - the subject of the working paper
  - the objective(s) of the work
  - the source of information used
  - how any sample was selected, and the actual sample size
  - the work done
  - the results obtained
  - analysis of errors or other significant observations
  - the conclusions drawn
  - the key points highlighted; and the need for any further work identified
  - All working papers should be neat, legible and clearly laid out; any diagrams should be clear and any abbreviations explained.

The main objective of having quality control guidelines is to ensure that any audit files can be picked up by any auditor and he should be able to understand it and should come to the same conclusion as the person who performed the work.

Review of audit work is also clearly important and this has been covered in a separate memorandum.

TASK 2(ii)

MEMORANDUM

TO: All Employees

FROM: Ruth Rolfe-Tarrant, Audit Senior   *REF:*   RRT/CWQual2

DATE: 15/4/X9

SUBJECT: Training Audit Staff; Monitoring and Reviewing Audit Work

Training of Audit Staff

Training is extremely important to ensuring that audit staff are sufficiently competent to perform the work required. It is clear that sufficient and relevant training forms part of the firm's overall quality control procedures (as per SAS 240). It is essential that all audit staff have the right qualifications and experience to perform the audit work which has been delegated to them. If they do not have those qualities then they should not perform the work. Where an auditor is lacking in skills it is important that this is recognised and appropriate action taken to ensure that those skills are acquired, otherwise a risk exists that the auditor may perform the work incompetently, may not notice something unusual, or may be unable to make informed conclusions on the results of any work. When recruiting staff, the audit firm should ensure that they are employing staff who are suitable for the relevant position, and that any further training requirements are taking account of and action taken to meet any skills gap.

At the end of every audit, a debriefing meeting is usually held which assesses how well the audit was conducted as a whole; one of the purposes of this is to improve the performance of individuals by identifying any areas of weakness and making provision for any training. The improvement of the conduct of future audits is also a purpose of the audit.

It is also important that the audit firm (and the individual themselves) ensures that they maintain an awareness and knowledge of current issues and developments within the industry so that they can ensure that they adhere to any new requirements and continue to offer the client a good service.

Monitoring and Reviewing Audit Work

As with training, both the monitoring and review functions are important in ensuring that the firm complies with its quality control procedures (as per SAS 240). It is not sufficient for a firm to just document and issue to staff a set of procedures to be performed, the firm must also monitor and review work to ensure that the procedures are being complied with.

In terms of monitoring, it is important that the progress of the audit as a whole is monitored in addition to the progress of individuals working on the audit. The following points should be considered by all staff supervising audits:

-   are the staff performing their assigned tasks competently
-   do they understand the work they are performing such that they would be able to identify any anomalies
-   are all staff carrying out their work in accordance with the overall audit plan and the audit programmes
-   are they kept informed at all times of any problems, and are they kept aware of any significant auditing and accounting issues and their resolution
-   are there any major differences of opinion which need to be addressed

It is vital that the audit (and individuals) are monitored on a timely basis to ensure that any problems can be identified and resolved such that the audit plan can be amended where necessary, any additional testing performed, and staff given assistance/training where required to ensure that the overall quality of the audit is maintained.

In respect of individual audits, and working papers the following points should be ensured at all times; and it is the responsibility of the person reviewing the work to ensure that this is achieved:

- that the work has been performed in line with the audit programme
- that the work performed and the results obtained have been adequately documented
- any significant matters have been resolved or are reflected in the audit conclusion
- all audit objectives have been achieved
- the conclusions are consistent with the results of the work performed and support the overall audit opinion.

After the audit senior has reviewed the work of the junior auditors a manager review followed by an engagement partner review will take place. The manager review will cover examination of some of the assistants' work, all of the senior's work and an overall review of the audit work. The engagement partner review looks at the manager's review, any controversial areas of the audit, the audit report etc

It is important that all reviews take place on a timely basis; clearly there is little point in the audit programmes being reviewed for adequacy after all the tests have been completed and the draft audit report prepared, they should be reviewed prior to the testing being performed. The key audit documentation which should be reviewed on a timely basis and prior to commencing the next stage of the audit are :

- the overall audit plan and the audit programmes
- the assessment of inherent and control risks
- systems documentation, and any conclusions from interviews performed
- the financial statements, any proposed adjustments
- the draft audit report.

TASK 3(i)

Client:	Diamond Dentists Ltd	**W/P REF**:	E1/1
Accounting Date:	31/03/X9		

Prepared By: RRT
Date: 21/4/X9
Reviewed By:
Date:

The internal control objectives being fulfilled if the controls as outlined in the ICQ exist and operate effectively are as follows:

1   *Are formal records maintained to ensure that all hours paid for are actually worked?*

The objective being satisfied is to ensure that all amounts recorded on the payroll records are for work actually performed.

2   *Does an appropriate person verify pay rates, overtime worked and gross pay calculations prior to wage payments being made?*

The objective being satisfied is to ensure that all amounts to be paid are accurate, and that no errors have been made.

3   *Are written notices required from an authorised individual prior to adding new employees to the payroll, and removing persons who have terminated their employment?*

The objective being satisfied is to ensure that only valid employees are paid, ie that non-existent employees are not paid nor are individuals paid for time prior to commencement of employment etc.

4   *Is authorisation required from all individuals prior to any payroll deductions (excluding statutory) being made?*

The objective being satisfied is to ensure that only valid deductions are made from any personnel's wage/salary.

5   *Are all employees required to sign for their wages prior to receiving them?*

The objective being satisfied is to ensure that wages are only received by the correct individual; this will also prevent anyone trying to claim twice ie stating that they hadn't received them.

6   *Are all payroll records held in a secure area only accessible by authorised individuals?*

The objective being satisfied is to ensure that only authorised individuals can access the confidential payroll information; this is especially important with the terms of the Data Protection Act.

7   *Does an appropriate official authorise pay rates?*

The objective being satisfied is that 'all elements of the payroll are authorised'. It is imperative that all elements of the payroll are authorised by someone suitably senior, and in some situations more than one person's authorisation may be required.

8   *Does the accounting system ensure the complete and accurate recording of payroll costs in the financial records?*

The objective being satisfied is that all elements of the payroll cost are completely and accurately recorded in the accounting records.

TASK 3(ii)

Client:	Diamond Dentists Ltd	**W/P REF**: F1/1
Accounting Date:	31/03/X9	

Prepared By: RRT
Date: 28/4/X9
Reviewed By:
Date:

AUDIT PROGRAMME: PAYROLL

AUDIT TEST	**W/P REF**	**WORK PERFORMED BY**
Control Tested: All payroll payments are valid (for work actually performed)		
1a Examine a sample of the timesheets and review the control over the timesheets to assess its adequacy		
1b Observe the time recording procedure on two occasions (these should be unannounced checks)		
1c Review the wages account and the payroll records for any large or unusual amounts		
Control Tested: Wages are correctly calculated and paid		
2a Examine documentary evidence of the internal verification of wages/salaries calculations		
2b Select a sample of timesheets and recalculate hours worked and agree to the payroll. Check that pay rates are correct and that formal documentation of pay rates has been authorised by the directors		
2c Recalculate gross pay for a sample of weeks (wages) and months (salaries) and agree to the payroll.		
Control Tested: Amounts on the payroll are for valid employees		
3a Identify exactly what the personnel policies are in respect of recruitment and termination		
3b Test a sample of entries on the payroll for authorisation of employment and termination of employment		
3c Compare a sample of initial/final payments made to the personnel records		
Control Tested: Only authorised deductions are made		
4a Assess and review the procedures for authorising payroll deductions		
4b Select a sample of individuals from the payroll who have made deductions and check these back to the evidence of authorisation given.		
Control Tested: Amounts are paid to the correct individual		
5a Observe the wages payout procedure		
5b Verify that individuals produce some type of identification prior to receiving their wages		

AUDIT TEST	W/P REF	WORK PERFORMED BY
Control Tested: Only authorised access to records is permitted 6a Identify where the payroll records are retained and assess whether or not this is a secure area ie are all cabinets locked; is the room locked when unoccupied and access denied to all other personnel during working hours except in special circumstances 6b Observe over the course of a day whether procedures are adhered to 6c Assess what confidentiality is provided when personnel records are temporarily required by non-payroll staff eg for appraisals		
Control Tested: All payroll amounts are authorised 7a Test a sample of entries on the payroll to the personnel files for authorisation of wage rates/salary amounts 7b Test a sample of details on the timesheets to the payroll, ensuring that rates of pay are correct		
Control Tested: All payroll transactions are accurately and completely recorded in the accounting records 8a Ascertain and review the procedures for recording all elements of the payroll 8b Select a sample of months and weeks and cast and cross cast the payroll, and trace postings to the wages and salaries accounts in the nominal ledger		

TASK 3(iii)

Possible consequences if the controls did not exist/were not operating effectively:

CONTROL	CONSEQUENCES IF NOT OPERATING EFFECTIVELY
1 All payroll payments are valid (for work actually performed)	Employees could be paid for work not performed and payroll costs would therefore be overstated.
2 Wages are correctly calculated and paid	Employees could be over or under paid and the payroll costs hence misstated.
3 Amounts on the payroll are for valid employees	Payments could be made to fictitious employees.
4 Only authorised deductions are made	Deductions could be taken from an individual without their consent and would have to be repaid on request at a loss to the business.
5 Amounts are paid to the correct individual	Amounts could be paid to unauthorised employees who could misappropriate the monies; the true employee would then have to be paid at a loss to the business.
6 Only authorised access to records is permitted	The Data Protection Act could be breached & 'distribution' of unauthorised information could have harmful consequences to the employee who could seek recompense from the business.
7 All payroll amounts are authorised	Employees could be over/under paid and the wages/salaries amount recorded would hence be misstated.
8 All payroll transactions are accurately and completely recorded in the accounting records	Payroll elements could be misstated in the accounting records and inaccurately stated in the financial statements.

TASK 4 (i)

Client:

Accounting Date:

W/P REF:
PREPARED BY: RRT
DATE: 1/4/X9
REVIEWED BY: GL
DATE: 5/4/X9

EVALUATION SCHEDULE

WEAKNESS	W/P REF	IMPLICATIONS	RECOMMENDATIONS
There is no separate log completed of amounts received, date/time, patient name, type of payment (i.e. cash/cheque) for reconciliation/control purposes. It is the sole responsibility of the dentist to record the relevant amount on to the patient's record on the PC (this is the only record of payment.)		All payments may not be recorded, and this would not be identified due to lack of reconciliation.	A separate independent log should be completed of amounts received and relevant details. This should then be reconciled to the dentists records on a regular basis such as weekly.
There is no check between the dentists' records and the actual monies received/paid in to the bank.		Amounts received from patients may not be being paid in to the bank and this would not be identified.	The paying in slips should be reconciled to the independent log (refer above point) by someone other than the person performing paying in duties.)
The dental technician performs dental repairs, is paid in cash yet the repair nor amount received is recorded.		Sales may be unrecorded and therefore the true sales amount would be understated and this would not be identified.	A repair note should be completed by the person receiving the repair prior to passing to the dental technician and then amounts paid centrally not to the Dental Technician separately.
Payments for sundry goods e.g. toothpaste etc are manually recorded by the person who accepts payment from the patient; who has responsibility for entering the sale on the patient's record.		There is a risk that such sales may not be recorded, and sales therefore understated.	All sundry goods should be receipted and paid through a cash till system; sums received should then be agreed to the till receipt at the end of each day.
Overall segregation of duties is weak; one person is often responsible for performing a number of functions ie accepting payment for treatment or goods, recording payments and		There is a risk that sales may not be recorded, or goods misappropriated due to the lack of controls, and this would not be identified.	Duties should be clearly segregated between the different staff who should indicate on the relevant documentation who performed the work and when.

◆ FOULKS*lynch*

Paying in the monies to the bank.					
Cash amounts received are placed in an unlocked, visible safe box throughout the day and is often left unattended.	Amounts could be misappropriated by staff, visitors or patients and this would not be identified.	The safe box should be kept locked at all times and out of visible sight and the keys held by nominated individuals only. At night the box should be placed in a secure environment.			
Cheques and cash are often retained on the premises for 2 to 3 days prior to being banked.	By retaining cash on the premises it increases the risk of theft. In addition the business is not taking full advantage of cashflow opportunities.	The firm should bank the money each day.			

TASK 4 (ii)

Carregan, Walters & Co
56 The High Street
St Maylow
Bruckingham
BN3 6HJ

Mr G Diamond
Diamond Dentists Ltd
Zandria Road
Bruckingham
BW1 6XY

Dear Mr Diamond

Regarding your queries in respect of the cash reconciliation I have outlined the points below which support the reasons and importance for a daily cash reconciliation:

At present there is no check between the 'cash' (ie both cash and cheques) received in a day and the actual amount that exists at the end of each day compared to that recorded on the computer system or the amounts paid in to the bank. This lack of controls means that cash could be easily misappropriated and this would not be detected. Although management accounts are produced on a monthly basis these cannot currently be relied upon as the accuracy of the sales figure is not certain – the accountant relies totally on the computer reports, however, these reports rely on the accuracy of the input by the receptionists. Due to the lack of segregation of duties the accuracy of input is not reliable.

The main type of sales receipts are cash and therefore the business must ensure that stringent controls are in place as clearly the risks attached to the security of cash are far higher than other forms of payment such as bank transfer.

A cash reconciliation should therefore be completed on a daily basis by someone other than the person who has been accepting cash payments and recording amounts on the computer system. The reconciliation should comprise agreeing the cash received in the day to the amount recorded on the computer system and this should be signed and dated by the person performing the reconciliation. The names of those persons involved in inputting and accepting cash receipts should also be documented. Any discrepancies should be investigated at the time of the count. In order to improve security cash should be deposited with the bank on a daily basis; the cash paying in slip should then be checked by an independent person such as the accountant to the daily cash reconciliation sheet. The daily reconciliation sheets should be retained and filed in date order so that they can be checked at any time – this would provide a useful means for the directors to perform spot checks to ensure that controls are being adhered to. It is important to remember that the directors of a company are solely responsible for the adequacy of the internal controls and their operation.

I hope these points clearly explain why a daily cash reconciliation is so important and the nature of such a reconciliation.

If you have any further queries or would like any further assistance in this matter please do not hesitate to contact me.

Yours sincerely

A Senior
Carregan, Walters & Co

TASK 4(iii)

Client:	Diamond Dentists Ltd	**W/P REF**:	F2/1
Accounting Date:	31/03/X9		

Prepared By: RRT
Date: 31/3/X9
Reviewed By:
Date:

AUDIT PROGRAMME: CASH BALANCES

AUDIT TEST	W/P REF	WORK PERFORMED BY	WORK REVIEWED BY
1	Record the time of the count and the staff present at the time of the count; also record the names of the audit staff conducting the count *Note: staff should not be informed of the count prior to the count taking place*			
2	Request that one of the staff present count the cash balance in the presence of the auditor(s) conducting the test. *Note: the auditor(s) should not be left alone with the cash at any time*			
3	Document the amount of the cash counted and analyse this clearly between the different types of notes and coins			
4	Document whether there are any IOUs or other similar 'documents' and the amount of these and the source. *Note: any IOUs should be followed up to ascertain whether or not these were approved and monies paid.*			
5	Obtain a report from the computer system detailing the 'sales' for the day and payment method.			
6	Check the last date of cash deposits to the bank account and check that the current cash balance agrees with the cash sales since then.			
7	Where 'sales' are for cheque, check that the cheques actually exist			
8	Review the financial statements to ensure that the correct cash balance is included			

Note: the date of the count should be as at the year end date ie 31/3/X9 especially due to the lack of internal controls

TASK 5

MEMORANDUM

TO: Susan Trollis

FROM: Ruth Rolfe-Tarrant, Audit Senior   *REF:*   RRT/STCC

DATE: 15/4/X9

SUBJECT: Computer Controls

Following your queries regarding computer controls, I have outlined below the difference between application controls and general controls. The two types of controls are very different and it is important that you consider them both separately and design tests accordingly. It is also important that you understand the link between the controls and therefore the implications of having weak controls of one type and how this affects the other type of control.

General Controls

General controls are those which exist over all the applications and relate to the environment within which computer based accounting systems are developed, maintained and operated, and which are therefore applicable to all the applications.   General controls exist to ensure the proper development and implementation of applications and the integrity of program and data files and of computer operations. General controls can be either manual or programmed.

Two examples of general controls are:

(i)   Physical controls such as keyboard locks, cardkey access to computer suites
(ii)   Back up controls to ensure continuity of operations eg back up every night with back up copies held off site.

Application Controls

These are controls which are specific to individual applications and relate to the transactions and standing data pertaining to each computer based accounting system and are therefore specific to each such application. Application controls may be manual or programmed and exist to ensure the accuracy of the accounting records resulting from both manual and programmed processing.

Two examples of application controls are:

(i)   use of control totals to ensure completeness of input, processing and output
(ii)   use of record counts and hash totals whenever master files are used to ensure that all records on the file have been processed.

TASK 5(ii)

Client:	Diamond Dentists Ltd
Accounting Date:	31 March 19X9

W/P REF:
PREPARED BY: RRT
REVIEWED BY:

WEAKNESS SCHEDULE

WEAKNESS	W/P REF	EFFECT/IMPLICATION	RECOMMENDATIONS
There is no virus checking software on the computer system at present.		All PCs could be infected in the event that a virus is inadvertently received by a third party – this could disrupt work and cause loss and damage to data which could be expensive to resolve	Not required
The PC with the accounts data can be accessed by anyone especially the Hygienist due to the password software being removed.		The accounts data could be erroneously changed – or data deleted or false information input (eg set up of dummy suppliers) and this may not be detected by the Accountant. This could ultimately result in loss of funds to the firm and fines in the event that false information was filed.	Not required
The dental technician does not currently use his system effectively, preferring to use a manual system		This does not ensure that records are complete and anyone wanting to obtain information from the system could not rely on it.	Not required
There are no physical access controls preventing unauthorised third party use.		The computer equipment could be damaged, stolen and/or confidential data obtained. This could result in loss to the firm in terms of time, inconvenience and breach of the Data Protection Act.	Not required
The password used is the same for all PCs i.e. '1234' and has never been changed.		Unauthorised persons could easily gain access to the data as the password is easily guessable and damage or steal the data; this would result in breach of the Data Protection Act.	Not required

WEAKNESSES	W/P REF	EFFECT/IMPLICATION	RECOMMENDATIONS
There is no one person controlling/supporting the use of the computer system, and dealing with problems/maintenance issues.		In the event of any problems encountered or damage the firm could end up paying large sums of money to have the issues resolved in the absence of any maintenance or support contract. In addition, the absence of one central person controlling the computer usage does not facilitate the best use of the system nor ensure that routines such as back ups are taken regularly.	Not required
There is no contingency plan in place stating what action would be in the event of a breakdown, theft or other disaster.		In the event of a 'disaster' Diamond Dentists would find it difficult to deal with the issues promptly and effectively; this could result in a loss of operations and an expensive/non appropriate solution being taken rather than one which is properly considered.	Not required
Back ups of data files are not taken on a regular basis.		Lack of back ups does not facilitate the timely recovery of data in the event of loss.	Not required
There does not appear to have been any specifc computer training performed.		Staff may not be using the system effectively or tailored to their requirements.	Not required

TASK 5(iii)

Computer Assisted Audit Techniques (CAATs) are ways in which the auditor can use a computer (either his own or the clients) to assist him in performing audit tests or assisting with his audit work.

The major different types of CAAT are as follows:

- *Audit Interrogation Software* – computer programs used for audit purposes to examine the content of the client's computer files. It typically performs tests which are usually done manually and involves examining large quantities of data for substantive testing. This alleviates the need for the auditor to spend extensive time on what is typically a routine task, thereby allowing him to concentrate on tasks which require more skill.

- *Test Data* – data used by the auditors for computer processing to test the operation of the client's computer programs. The test data is set up by the auditor who documents the expected results, submits the data and then compares the actual to expected results which should be identical.

- *Embedded Audit Facilities* – these are entities or elements set up the auditor on the client's computer system. They facilitate the possibility of continuous checking of data over a period. An embedded facility consists of audit modules that are incorporated into the computer element of the enterprise's accounting system. Two commonly used methods are Integrated Test Facility (ITF) and Systems Control and Review File (SCARF). For example, the auditor could set up a fictitious customer within the purchase ledger and transactions are then posted to that entity during normal processing and actual results compared to expected results.

CAATs could be used to test the creditor information in the following ways:

The samples could be selected using CAATs to ensure that the sample is statistical and therefore can be supported as valid.

CAATs could be used to set up dummy creditors and then have information posted to that supplier in the same way as normal suppliers and then check the actual to the expected results.

CAATs could be used to run interrogations against the dentists system to obtain information in respect of creditors such as purchases in the year, returned goods, aged creditor information etc

CAATs could be used to run substantive tests against the creditor information which would be predefined and then compare the actual to the expected results.

Test data could be set up and posted to the creditors accounts and then actual results compared to actual – it would have to be ensured that the information was deleted after the tests had been completed; or alternatively a copy of the system could be taken and used separately by the auditor.

TASK 6(i)

Client:	Diamond Dentists Ltd	**W/P REF**:	F1/1
Accounting Date:	31/03/X9		

Prepared By: RRT
Date: 28/4/X9
Reviewed By:
Date:

Purpose of the Overall Review:

The overall review of the financial statements conducted at the end of the audit is an extremely important part of the audit process and is performed for the following reasons:

1   It is recommended by SAS 470 and is therefore best practice which should be adhered to in order to ensure that the auditor can prove that he has properly conducted the audit should such an occasion be necessary. SAS 470 states that 'the auditor should carry out such a review of the financial statements as is sufficient, in conjunction with the conclusions drawn from the other audit evidence obtained, to give them a reasonable basis for their opinion on the financial statements.

2   It enables the auditor to be confident that the audit opinion that he has arrived at is correct in line with the results from his other audit testing. He should gain the same opinion from performing his overall review (including analytical procedures) as that which he has obtained from the evidence of his other audit tests.

3   To ensure that the accounting policies used by the client are in line with statutory requirements, and that the accounting policies employed are in accordance with the accounting standards, are properly disclosed, consistently applied and are appropriate to the client. The auditor would consider factors such as:
  • the policies commonly used within the industry
  • whether the financial statements reflect the true substance of the relevant transactions and not necessarily their form
  • whether the financial statements show a true and fair view, or whether a departure from Generally Accepted Accounting Principles is necessary in the circumstances

4   To check for consistency and reasonableness. The financial statements should adequately reflect the information and explanations received during the course of the audit. Checks performed should highlight any anomalies / factors which should be highlighted to the user to ensure a proper understanding of the financial statements.

5   To consider the impact of aggregate uncorrected misstatements identified during the course of the audit and whether any adjustments are necessary.

TASK 6(ii)

Client:	Diamond Dentists Ltd	**W/P REF**:	F1/1
Accounting Date:	31/03/X9		

Prepared By: RRT
Date: 28/4/X9
Reviewed By:
Date:

Overall Review - Checks to be Performed on Diamond Dentists Ltd Financial Statements

The checks to be performed are as followed:

1   An examination of the accounting policies used to ensure that these are consistent with previous years or where they have changed that such changes are appropriate.

2   To consider whether the equipment that has been hired has been correctly reflected within the financial statements.

3   Analytical Review to ensure that the financial statements as a whole are consistent with the knowledge of the business; this typically comprises ratios which would be as follows:

- Accounting ratios which examine factors such as liquidity, profitability and gearing (see 'Note 1' below)
- Comparisons with other similar firms
- Comparisons with industry averages
- Comparisons with previous years

4   Examine any significant fluctuations or unexpected relationships which are inconsistent with other information or deviate from expected patterns

5   Review profit and loss account expenditure items to ensure that:
- Rent is in line with the lease agreement
- Rates are in line with the rates notification
- Hire charges are in line with the hire agreement
- The overdraft agreement was complied with (and establish whether an agreed overdraft limit still exists even though Diamond Dentists is now in a positive cash situation
- Check that purchases costs reflect the increases in line with the firms increase in income
- Check that staff costs have increased in line with written salary/wage agreements.

6   Check the actual costs to the budget for the year and identify any significant variations and obtain explanations for such variances.

Ratios to be Calculated:

1   Gross Profit Percentage:

$$\frac{\text{Gross Profit}}{\text{Sales}} \ \times 100\% = \frac{85,000}{115,000} \ \times 100\% = 73.9\%$$

2   Debtors Turnover:

$$\frac{\text{Sales}}{\text{Debtors}} = \frac{115,000}{200} = 575 \text{ times}$$

This is clearly an extremely large number as the amount of debtors is so small and therefore not worth monitoring closely.

3   Stock Turnover:

$$\frac{\text{Cost of sales}}{\text{Stock}} = \frac{20,000}{4,000} = 5 \text{ times}$$

4   Current Ratio:

$$\frac{\text{Current Assets}}{\text{Current Liabilities}} = \frac{47,200}{4,500} = 10.5:1$$

5   Quick Ratio / Acid Test:

$$\frac{\text{Current Assets - Stock}}{\text{Current Liabilities}} = \frac{43,200}{4,500} = 9.6:1$$

6   Gearing:

$$\frac{\text{Long term Liabilities}}{\text{Share Capital \& Reserves}} \ \times 100\% = \frac{25,000}{68,700} = 36\%$$

7   Return on Capital Employed:

$$\frac{\text{Profitre before Tax}}{\text{Total Assets less Current Liabilities}} \ \times 100\% = \frac{10,400}{93,700} = 11\%$$

Note: There are an extensive range of ratios that could be calculated; it is important that the student calculates a balanced range of ratios which include those relating to profitability, liquidity and gearing

TASK 7

Management Letter Extract:

Carregan, Walters & Co
56 The High Street
St Maylow
Bruckingham
BN3 6HJ

The Directors
Diamond Dentists Ltd
Zandria Road
Bruckingham
BW1 6XY

PRIVATE AND CONFIDENTIAL

15th June 20X9

Dear Sirs

Diamond Dentists Ltd

Audit for the year ended 31 March 20X9

In accordance with our normal practice, we are writing to you with regard to matters arising out of our audit for the year ended 31 March 20X9 which we consider should be brought to your attention.

Our responsibilities as auditors are governed by the Companies Act and principally require us to report on the accounts laid before the company in general meeting.

This report has been prepared for the sole use of the directors of Diamond Dentists Ltd. None of its contents may be disclosed to third parties without our written consent. Carregan, Walters & Co assumes no liability to any other persons.

The matters detailed in this report reflect matters coming to our attention during the course of our audit. They are not intended to be a comprehensive statement of all weaknesses that may exist or of all improvements that could be made. We set out below within Section A those matters which we consider to be of fundamental importance. Other matters of lesser significance, but which still require your attention, are dealt with in Section B.

Section A

(a)   *Stock Records*

There are no formalised records maintained of the Dentists stocks of teeth. It is therefore impossible for him to ascertain at any point in time how many of any particular stock item he has and therefore he cannot ensure that he maintains adequate levels at all times; this could result in delays in job completion whilst awaiting stock deliveries. Management accounts produced throughout the year cannot be relied upon due to the lack of stock control throughout the year – the only time that the stock figure is correct is at year end when the annual stocktake is performed.

Recommendation

Formalised stock records should be established detailing current stock levels and maximum, minimum and re-order levels should be established. Documented orders should then be prepared on a regular basis such as fortnightly and placed direct with Teethright via fax or email (Teethright should be contacted to obtain predesigned order forms). Deliveries should be checked against the order and the invoice to ensure consistency and the stock records updated accordingly; any out of stock items should be noted for re-order.

(b)   Delivery/Invoice Controls

At present there is no check against the actual items delivered to the invoice to ensure that the amount charged is correct; Diamond Dentists Ltd could be overcharged ie for goods not received and this would not be detected. It is not currently possible to check to an order form as none exist and therefore goods could be delivered which have not been ordered resulting in higher than required stock levels.

Recommendation

By implementing recommendation in point (a) this will ensure that invoices are checked to delivery notes and orders; invoices should then only be paid for goods actually received.

(c)   Existence of Gold Stocks

There are currently no records of gold stocks maintained nor is there any figure for such stocks included within the financial statements. The balance sheet assets are therefore understated by £1,950.

Recommendation

Formalised records as for stocks of teeth (see point (a) of this letter) should be established and maintained up to date. The financial statements should be amended such that stocks are increased by £1,950.

Section B

(a)   Security of Gold stocks

The stocks of gold are currently held in an unlocked drawer and could easily be misappropriated by any of the staff, a patient or an opportunist thief who has gained access to the dental laboratory which is unlocked and also accessible by an external door. Due to the lack of records maintained (refer Section A point (c)) any such misappropriations would not be identified. Although the amount is not material in terms of total assets it represents a sufficient value to warrant adequate security.

Recommendation

Stocks of gold should be held in a secure safe box in a locked cabinet when not in use and the keys held by a limited number of authorised staff. In addition the dental laboratory should be locked when not occupied, and the external door should only be unlocked when its use is required.

TASK 8(i)

MEMORANDUM

TO: Susan Trollis

FROM: Ruth Rolfe-Tarrant, Audit Senior   *REF:*   RRT/STAR

DATE: 30/6/X9

SUBJECT: Audit Reports

The unqualified audit report includes the following sections:

1   It is headed 'Auditor's report to the shareholders of xxx Ltd'

2   Paragraph 1 of the report states that the auditors have audited the financial statements and it gives the pages which the audit report covers. It states the accounting convention used which is usually the historic cost convention. It also states where the accounting policies can be found within the financial statements.

3   Paragraph 2 states the directors' and auditors' responsibilities, although the directors responsibilities are usually detailed on a separate page within the financial statements and referred to within the audit report.

4   Paragraph 3 describes the audit procedures used in the conduct of the audit, including the following key points:
   • The audit is conducted in accordance with accounting standards
   • Transactions are examined on a test basis
   • Estimates and judgements made by the firm are examined
   • The auditors consider whether the accounting policies are appropriate, consistently applied and adequately disclosed
   • The auditor obtains sufficient, relevant and reliable evidence to support audit conclusions that there are no material misstatements
   • That misstatements include fraud, irregularity and error
   • The auditor considers whether the presentation of the financial information is adequate.

5   The final paragraph is the audit opinion which is qualified or unqualified and refers to the financial statements and the Companies Act 1985.

6   The audit report ends with the firm's name and address ie 'Carregan, Walters & Co', the fact that they are registered auditors and the date. The date is usually the same as the date when the directors approve and sign the financial statements.

TASK 8(ii)

Taking into consideration the points outlined in SAS600; the form of audit report that would be given in the two scenarios outlined by Susan are as follows:

Weakness 1

The problems detected clearly result in an uncertainty as it is impossible due to the total lack of evidence to identify the amount of cash sales. It would clearly not therefore be appropriate to give an unqualified opinion as the effect of the misstatement is so material that the figure for cash sales cannot be verified as to its, so a qualified option – 'except for ….. would be given. With this form of audit report the opinion paragraph would be as follows:

Qualified Opinion arising from limitation of in auditor's scope.

Except for any adjustments that might have been found to be necessary had we been able to obtain sufficient evidence concerning cash sales, in our opinion the financial statements give a true and fair view of the state of the company's affairs as at 31 March 20X9 and of its profit for the year then ended and have been properly prepared in accordance with the Companies Act 1985.

In respect of the limitation on our work relating to cash sales:

(a)   We have not obtained all the information and explanations that we considered necessary for the purposes of our audit, and

(b)   We were unable to determine whether proper accounting records had been maintained

Weakness 2

3% of the value of the fixed assets held by Diamond Dentists are no longer used even though they were only bought in April 1998 – they were found to be impractical and unusable within the industry and therefore are now obsolete as no-one is willing to buy them. Diamond Dentists however, are still holding the items at their full value (cost less one year's depreciation) in the financial statements.

In the case of weakness 2 the financial statements are affected by a fundamental uncertainty ie the value of tangible fixed assets. In this situation I would recommend that the nature and amount of the uncertainty is disclosed within the financial statements so that the financial statements do actually give a true and fair view. If the directors are willing to accept the additional disclosure then an unqualified opinion could be given with an explanatory paragraph. The explanatory paragraph would be as follows (and would appear immediately before the opinion paragraph):

Fundamental Uncertainty

An uncertainty exists as to the value of tangible fixed assets as there is some doubt as to whether the fall in the current value of the assets is permanent or temporary. Our opinion is not qualified in this respect.

Audit Opinion

The audit opinion would read the same as that for an unqualified report.

TASK 9

Carregan, Walters & Co
56 The High Street
St Maylow
Bruckingham
BN3 6HJ

Mr G Diamond
Diamond Dentists Ltd
Zandria Road
Bruckingham
BW1 6XY

17 July 20X9

Dear Mr Diamond

Further to your claim that our firm should have identified the fraud during the course of the audit and have therefore been negligent I feel that I should clarify the following points regarding the auditor's responsibilities for detecting fraud and error in the financial statements.

The auditing standards clearly state that the auditor should design his audit procedures so that he has a reasonable expectation of detecting material fraud or error. It is important to stress that the key point is 'materiality'. The auditor performs his work on a sample basis and does not check every item in the financial statements; he cannot be expected to identify every instance of fraud only those which materially affect the financial statements. An exception to this rule is where the fraud has been concealed and it is unreasonable for the auditor to detect such fraud – clearly this would be a point for the courts to decide.

The auditor is unlikely to be held negligent for not detecting an immaterial fraud, however, there are exceptions to this rule; these are as follows:

- If the auditor detects such a fraud whilst performing his normal audit procedures and fails to report it to the client's management

- If the auditor carries out audit procedures on immaterial items and these procedures are not performed satisfactorily and therefore fail to detect the fraud

- If the auditor performs audit procedures on immaterial items at the specific request of the client's management and fails to detect an immaterial fraud due to negligent work.

In these three cases the client would have a good case for claiming damages against negligence against the auditor.

In respect of your claim of negligence I would like to make the following points:

the fraud amounted to £420; this represents 4% of the company's profit before tax and is therefore immaterial. However, as the auditor performed work on cash sales and it was clearly highlighted as an area of weakness it could be argued that the auditor should have detected the fraud. However, it could also be argued that the company has a responsibility for allowing the fraud to take place, as there was clearly serious weaknesses within the company's internal controls, ie there should have been proper segregation of duties and accounting controls in place. In addition, it could also be argued that the auditors had clearly recommended within the previous year's management letter that a cash reconciliation should be performed and this has not yet been actioned. If such controls had been put into place after last year's audit the fraud could have been prevented.

Taking all these points into consideration I therefore do not consider that as auditors we have performed our task negligently, however, I would suggest that the controls previously suggested and reiterated at this year's audit should now be put into place and we would be willing to work with you to achieve this.

I look forward to meeting with you to discuss this matter; in the interim if you have any further queries please do not hesitate to contact me.

Yours sincerely

A Partner
Carregan, Walters & Co

CLASS ACTIVITIES

QUESTIONS

Chapters 1–2
FRAMEWORK OF AUDITING

---

1 Activity

You are an Audit Partner for a firm of accountants who have just been accepted as auditors of a new client Buggies Ltd. The initial meeting with the client was held yesterday and an extract from the meeting is shown below:

Client: Buggies Ltd	**WP Ref:**	**A1/1**
	Prepared by:	**AS**
	Date:	**30/6/X8**
	Reviewed by:	**SLA**
	Date:	**5/7/X8**

Extract

Meeting with Buggies Ltd

Present: A Smith, Audit Partner
F Bloggs, Managing Director, Buggies Ltd
S Brown, Finance Director, Buggies Ltd

Date: 30 June 20X8

Address (and Registered Office) of Buggies Ltd
2 Dean Road
London
WC1 6XY.

Financial Year End
31st July

Number of Employees
400

Directors
F Bloggs, Managing Director
S Brown, Finance Director
F Meek, Personnel Director
G Harolds, Sales Director

The scope of the audit was discussed, which the Audit Partner stated would be confirmed within the letter of engagement.

During the meeting F Bloggs requested that your firm also completed their VAT return for them each quarter and reviewed their current management accounting system for them and made recommendations as to how it could be improved.

The fees were only mentioned briefly as these had been discussed in detail prior to the firm's acceptance as auditors.

F Bloggs also mentioned that the previous auditors had been asked to leave as the Finance Director had identified a fraud in the previous year which the auditors had not picked up; he considered this to be a significant failing on their part.

Task 1

Draft a letter of engagement to be sent to Buggies Ltd.

Task 2

Explain why a letter of engagement is desirable for the auditor.

Chapters 3–4

COMPANIES ACTS REQUIREMENTS

---

1   Activity

You have just started working for a small firm of accountants and the first audit which you will be assisting on is the company where your sister works as a Financial Director. Whilst in the planning meeting the audit manager is discussing independence and you are unsure as to exactly whether or not this relationship prevents you from performing any audit work. When discussing this with the manager he suggests you do some reading on the subject to aid your understanding and continue the discussion the next day.

He also provides you with details of personal circumstances of other audit staff and asks you to consider what the outcome should be (see extract below).

Extract

(i)   One of the audit partners is a personal friend of the chief accountant of Ponters Ltd. The chief accountant is not a director of the company and the audit partner is not responsible for Ponters Ltd's work.

(ii)   The audit fee receivable from Ticko plc is £150,000; the total fee income of the audit firm is £700,000.

(iii)   The audit senior in charge of the audit of Goldies Bank has a personal loan from the bank of £5,000 on which he is paying the market interest rate.

(iv)   One of the partners is responsible for two audits, H Ltd and J Ltd. H Ltd has recently tendered for a contract with J Ltd for a supply of material quantities of goods over a number of years. J Ltd has asked the audit partner to advise on the matter.

Task 1

Prepare a memorandum addressed to the audit manager explaining what is meant by independence and suggest ways in which the auditor can try and ensure his independence is maintained.

Conclude on whether you think your relationship prevents you from assisting on the audit.

Task 2

State what you think the outcome should be in each of the four situations in the extract provided to you by the audit manager.

Chapter 5

AUDIT APPOINTMENT

1	Activity

Growfast plc was formed on 1 August 20X0 in order to manufacture minicomputers. The directors are unsure as to their responsibilities, and the nature of their relationship with the external auditors. The audit partner has asked you as audit manager to visit the client and explain to the directors the more fundamental aspects of the accountability of the company and their relationship with the auditor.

Task

Prior to your meeting the audit partner asks you to write a letter to the directors of Growfast plc explaining the following points in your letter, which will be discussed at the meeting:

1. Why an audit is required
2. How the auditor of a public company may be appointed under the CA85
3. What the auditor's rights are under the CA85
4. The responsibilities of the directors in relation to the accounting function of the company.

Chapter 6

PLANNING THE AUDIT

1 Activity

Arnold Ltd is a long established family company which manufactures cosmetics. These are sold to customers who package and market them under their own tradenames. The company has three manufacturing units in Hull, Norwich and Cardiff.

The company has recently undergone some management changes following the death of its elderly managing director. Gill Hadden, formerly the sales director, is the new managing director. A new sales director, from outside the company, has been appointed.

The finance director and company accountant, Dick Patel, is 65 and has recently negotiated a part-time contract of employment with the company. The company will appoint a full-time accountant to replace Dick after the next financial year end.

Profits have declined in the last two years and the company is seeking to improve profitability prior to a possible listing on the Alternative Investment Market . An incentive scheme has recently been implemented with the aim of improving productivity within the company. Certain managers, and all the directors, will be paid a bonus based on production achieved above a predetermined level.

You are the audit senior for the audit of Arnold Ltd and you are about to commence planning for the audit.

Two of the firm's junior auditors will be assisting you on the audit and you have recently briefed them on the background of Arnold Ltd to assist with their understanding of the audit. They were somewhat confused over the difference between some of the audit terms you were using in relation to risk and you have asked them to refer to the firm's methodology as you are very busy; however you are aware that this is inadequate in some areas and may need updating.

Task 1

The new managing director has approached you and asked you to clarify some audit terms for her which she read about in a recent magazine article.

Write her a letter explaining the following terms:

- Audit risk (including a brief explanation of the audit risk formula)
- Inherent risk
- Control risk
- Detection risk.

Task 2

Prepare a working paper for inclusion in the planning section of the current audit file for Arnold Ltd which details the factors which should be considered when assessing the inherent risk of the company. Include within your working paper an overall conclusion as to whether you consider the inherent risk to be high, medium or low.

Chapters 7–8

INTERNAL CONTROLS AND AUDIT TESTING

---

1   Activity

Your firm of accountants audits a company which deals in properties. Among its properties is a vacant city centre site which, owing to local planning regulations, will not be developed for at least three years. The directors of the company have decided to use the vacant site (which they have enclosed) as a car park for up to 200 vehicles at any one time. Your firm has been asked to prepare a report on systems of control which would be appropriate in the operation of such a car park.

The company intends to operate the car park as follows:

Hours of business

Monday to Saturday 0600 hours to 2200 hours (site locked with exits and entrances barred between 2200 hours and 0600 hours and all day Sunday).

Charges	Length of stay		
Scale of charges	up to 1 hour	-	£0.20
	1 - 2 hours	-	£0.40
	2 - 3 hours	-	£0.60
	up to maximum of 16 hours	-	£3.20
	overnight stay	-	£2.00

Staffing

Number of attendants - 4 with only one attendant working at any one time on one shift either 0600-1400 or 1400-2200 hours. (Each attendant normally works 4 days per week, thus allowing for holidays and illness.)

Operating details

All cars to enter past one automatic barrier and machine which issues a date and time-stamped entry ticket to the car driver.

All cars to leave through one manned exit barrier after paying the attendant the correct fee.

Staff work routine

Members of staff on early shift from 0600 to 1400 hours must unlock exit and entrance and pay booth. At the beginning of either shift the member of staff must ensure:

(i)   that there are sufficient pre-numbered tickets in the ticket machine;

(ii)   that the correct date and time are being printed by the ticket machine;

(iii)   that the correct cash float (£20) is in the pay booth till.

When cars leave, duration of stay and fee are calculated and entered by the staff member on the pre-numbered ticket issued by the ticket machine. The correct fee is received by the attendant, who retains the pre-numbered ticket.

At the end of the shift all cash received should be either banked (day shift) or deposited in the night safe (night shift) by the appropriate attendant and cash float of £20 retained. The pay booth must be securely locked when the car park is closed and during any short absence of an attendant. During the afternoon a member of accounts department staff from head office collects all used tickets and records of cash banked. All accounting records are maintained at head office.

Task 1

Write a letter to the company directors describing types of internal control which could be used to achieve the objective of 'completeness of income'.

Task 2

Prepare an audit programme detailing two tests of control you would perform to ensure that income is complete.

Task 3

Explain why the tests (in Task 2) will give you this assurance ie, completeness of income.

Chapter 9

SAMPLING

---

1 Activity

Healthy Milk Ltd buys milk from dairy farmers, processes the milk and delivers it to retail outlets. You are currently auditing the debtors system and determine the following information:

(i) The company employs 75 drivers who are each responsible for delivering milk to customers. Each driver delivers milk to between 20 and 30 shops on a daily basis. Debtors normally amount to approximately £450,000. Payments by customers are not normally made to the drivers but are sent directly to the head office of the company.

(ii) The sales ledger is regularly reviewed by the office manager who prepares a list for each driver of accounts with 90 day balances or older. This list is used for the purpose of intensive collection by the drivers. Each driver has a delivery book which is used for recording deliveries of milk and those debtors with 90 day balances.

Having reviewed the debtors system for the audit of the financial year ended 31/3/X8, you conclude that statistical sampling techniques should be used to assist your audit work.

You also reviewed the previous year's audit file and identified that in previous years the test used was 'to select two accounts from each driver's customers, one to be chosen by opening each driver's delivery book at random and the other as the fourth item on the list of 90 day or older accounts'; (each page of the driver's delivery book deals with a single customer). You consider however, that this method would not produce a valid statistical sample. The junior auditor assisting you with the work tells you that in his opinion there is no point in using statistical sampling techniques as they do not relieve the auditor of his responsibilities in the exercise of his professional judgement.

On the completion of your review and testing of the 2,000 debtor balances, your statistical sample of 100 accounts disclosed 10 errors. You therefore conclude that there must be 200 accounts in the entire population which are in error as you are sure that the errors detected in the sample will be in exact proportion to the errors in the population.

Task 1

Explain to the junior auditor why the previous year's audit approach would not produce a valid statistical sample.

Task 2

Prepare a working paper for inclusion in the current audit file stating the audit objectives in selecting a sample of 90 day accounts for direct confirmation.

Task 3

As Audit Senior draft a suitable reply to the junior auditor's comment that 'there is no point in using statistical sampling techniques as they do not relieve the auditor of his responsibilities in the exercise of his professional judgement'.

Chapters 10–12

AUDIT OF STOCKS AND FIXED ASSETS

1 Activity

You have been appointed auditor of Brown Leasing plc which was formed fifteen years ago to lease construction equipment to road contractors and you are about to commence the interim audit. The company has 1,150 pieces of equipment on three-year operating leases to 300 customers. Brown Leasing plc is responsible for the repair and maintenance of the equipment and the economic life of the equipment normally averages six years. At the end of the lease period, the contractors can purchase the equipment at the market value of the equipment. If the equipment is not sold to the contractor, it is sold by auction. The company keeps a computerised plant register, and a separate manual record which both detail the description, cost, contractor-lessee, and rental payment. The managing director of the company has a reputation for expensive personal tastes and for shrewd, sometimes unethical, business dealings. However, it appears that the managing director enjoys a good reputation with his clients who often make their cheques payable to him. If this occurs, the managing director endorses them over to the company; this procedure causes you some concern and the audit partner has asked you to pay particular attention to this area during your testing.

Task 1

As Audit Senior, prepare an audit programme detailing the tests you would perform to verify the construction equipment out on lease for financial year ended 31/3/X8.

Task 2

Prepare an audit programme detailing the tests you would perform to verify the sales of equipment at the end of the lease period.

Task 3

Write a memorandum to the Audit Partner detailing the further action you think should be taken in respect of the situation with the Managing Director endorsing customer cheques; although your audit tests did not reveal any fraudulent activity your suspicions have been further aroused by conversations you have overheard during the course of the audit.

Chapter 13

AUDIT OF DEBTORS AND CASH

1	Activity

You are the partner in charge of the audit of Bon Voyage Ltd, a company which runs a travel agency business through a head office in London and ten retail shops spread throughout the country, six of which have been opened during the last year. A medium-term bank loan was negotiated to cover the additional working capital required for this expansion. Summarised balance sheet extracts for the years ended 30 November 20X5 and 20X4 are as follows:

	20X5		20X4	
	£	£	£	£
Tangible assets*:				
Fixed assets		163,000		199,000
Current assets:				
Trade debtors and				
prepayments	197,500		141,400	
Bank	37,600		41,200	
Cash (floats, unbanked cash,				
travellers' cheques)	67,000		52,500	
	302,100		235,100	
Creditors:				
Trade creditors, customers				
deposits and sundry				
accruals	166,200		146,400	
Net current assets		135,900		88,700
Total assets less current liabilities		298,900		207,700
Creditors: amounts falling due after				
more than one year:				
Bank loan		60,000		-
		238,900		207,700

*   A tangible fixed asset is one that physically exists and can be touched.

As partner in charge of the audit you are concerned as to the extent and quality of the audit work performed by your firm.

Task 1

Draft a typical standard bank letter to be used in the audit.

Task 2

Prepare a working paper to form part of the planning section of the current audit file providing guidance to the auditors who will be conducting the work stating the evidence required for the following balance sheet items:

- Bank and bank loans

- Cash (floats, unbanked cash and travellers' cheques).

Chapter 14

AUDIT OF LIABILITIES

1   Activity

Auditors carry out certain procedures during their audit work to ensure that assets are not overstated and liabilities are not understated in the balance sheet.

You are the audit senior carrying out the audit (year end 31/12/X5) of Oxton Electrical Wholesalers Ltd, who sell electrical products to retail stores. The products they sell include record, tape and compact disc players, television, video recorders, radios, microwave ovens and magnetic tapes for video and audio recorders and players. All of their purchases are made on credit; terms are usually 30 days . The draft figure in the financial statements for creditors is twice the amount as at last year, yet turnover has remained constant.

Task 1

Prepare an outline audit programme detailing those tests to be performed to ensure that trade creditors and accruals are not understated as at the year end 31/12/X5.

Task 2

Issue a memo to the remainder of the audit team explaining why it is more difficult to ensure that current liabilities are not understated, than it is to ensure that assets are not overstated.

One of the junior auditors has also commented that 'it is important for an auditor to ensure that assets are not overstated and liabilities are not understated in the balance sheet', he then continued that in his opinion 'it is more serious to overstate profit than understate it'.

Discuss these comments in your memo.

Chapter 15

COMPUTERS IN AUDIT

1 Activity

You are the auditor of Oilco plc, a major petroleum refiner, and you are about to commence the interim audit. The company utilises an on-line computerised accounting system operated by a central mainframe computer with terminals located in several departments. The audit senior has asked you to take charge of the interim audit of sales and debtors, and has arranged a meeting between yourself and the accountant responsible for the debtors section.

The audit senior further informs you that he wishes you to review the controls in existence not only as regards the accounting for sales and debtors but also the database facility as far as it concerns your audit assignment, and has scheduled an additional meeting with the Database Manager.

Task 1

List ten questions to ask the accountant at the scheduled meeting to enable you to make an initial evaluation of the effectiveness of the computer controls over sales and debtors.

Task 2

In preparation for your meeting with the Database Manager, detail the controls which you consider should be in existence in order to maintain the integrity of the Database.

Task 3

Following your meeting with the Database Manager you were somewhat confused with some of the terms he used which he informed you related to recent technological improvements. After requesting some relevant training, the Audit Partner has asked you to write him a memorandum explaining why you consider it so important to constantly keep up to date with the latest developments, and how often you consider such training to be required.

Chapters 16–18

THE FINAL AUDIT

1 Activity

You are currently engaged in reviewing the working papers of several audit assignments recently carried out by your audit practice. Each of the audit assignments is nearing completion, but certain matters have recently come to light which may affect your audit opinion on each of the assignments. In each case the year end of the company is 30 September 20X8.

(a) **Jones Ltd** (Profit before tax £150,000)

On 3 October 20X8 a letter was received informing the company that a debtor, who owed the company £30,000 as at the year end had been declared bankrupt on 30 September. At the time of the audit it was expected that unsecured creditors, such as Jones Ltd, would receive nothing in respect of this debt. The directors refuse to change the accounts to provide for the loss, on the grounds that the notification was not received by the balance sheet date.

Total debts shown in the balance sheet amounted to £700,000.

(b) **Roberts Ltd** (Profit before tax £500,000)

On 31 July 20X8 a customer sued the company for personal damages arising from an unexpected defect in one of its products. Shortly before the year end the company made an out-of-court settlement with the customer of £10,000, although this agreement is not reflected in the financial statements as at 30 September 20X8. Further, the matter subsequently became known to the press and was extensively reported. The company's legal advisers have now informed you that further claims have been received following the publicity, although they are unable to place a figure on the potential liability arising from such claims which have not yet been received. The company had referred to the claims in a note to the financial statements stating, however, that no provision had been made to cover them because the claims were not expected to be material.

(c) **Williams plc** (Net loss for the year £75,000)

Three directors of this manufacturing company owed amounts totalling £50,000 at the end of the financial year, and you have ascertained that such loans were not of a type permissible under the Companies Act 1985. These amounts had been included in the balance sheet with other items under the heading 'Debtors collectable within one year'. The directors did not wish to disclose these loans separately in the accounts as they were repaid shortly after the year end, as soon as they were made aware that the loans were not permissible. The directors have argued that the disclosures could prove embarrassing and that no purpose would be served by revealing this information in the accounts.

(d)   **Griffiths Ltd** (Net profit before tax £250,000)

The audit work revealed that a trade investment stated in the balance sheet at £500,000 had suffered a permanent fall in value of £300,000. The company admitted that the loss had occurred, but refused to make a provision for it on the grounds that other trade investments (not held for resale) had risen in value and were stated at amounts considerably below their realisable values.

Task

Prepare a memorandum addressed to the other partners in the firm informing them of the problems of each case. You should refer to materiality considerations and, where appropriate, relevant accounting principles and appropriate accounting standards. You should also indicate, with reasons, the kind of audit report (including the type of qualification, if necessary) which you consider would be appropriate in each case.

You are not required to produce the full audit reports, and you may assume that all matters other than those specifically mentioned are considered satisfactory.

Chapters 19–20

AUDITOR'S LIABILITY AND CURRENT ISSUES

1   Activity

You are one of the audit partners in a firm of auditors and a local radio company has approached you for an interview on the subject of fraud. Prior to the interview they have asked you to prepare a discussion paper for them to read out extracts to the listeners to stimulate interest in the interview.

Task

Prepare a discussion paper commenting whether it is practical and desirable, within the limits of procedures and costs, for the auditor to accept a general responsibility to detect fraud and other irregularities.

◈ FOULKS*lynch*   AAT

FOULKS LYNCH
4 The Griffin Centre
Staines Road
Feltham
Middlesex, TW14 0Hs
United Kingdom

OTLINES: Telephone: +44 (0) 20 8831 9990
Fax: +44 (0) 20 8831 9991
E-mail: info@foulkslynch.com

For information and online ordering, please visit our website at:
www. foulkslynch.com

ODUCT RANGE

r publications cover all assessments for the AAT standards competence.

r AAT product range consists of:

Textbooks	£10.50	Workbooks	£10.50
Combined Textbooks/Workbooks	£10.50	Lynchpin	£6.25

THER PUBLICATIONS FROM FOULKS LYNCH

e publish a wide range of study material in the accountancy field and specialize in texts for the following ofessional qualifications:

Chartered Institute of Management Accountants (CIMA)
Association of Chartered Certified Accountants (ACCA)
Certified Accounting Technicians (CAT)

OR FURTHER INFORMATION ON OUR PUBLICATIONS:

would like information on publications for: ACCA ❑   AAT ❑
                                                CAT ❑   CIMA ❑

Please keep me updated on new publications: ❑   By E-mail ❑   By Post ❑

Your Name...   Your email address.....................................
Your address:...
....
....
....

Prices are correct at time of going to press and are subject to change